Spider's Web

MEMOIRS OF
NORMAN "SPIDER" WEISS

TC SC

LAW

Triangle

Germany

West Point

Pennsylvania

Daytona Beach   NAPLES

To order additional copies of this book, contact:
Xlibris Corporation
1-888-795-4274
www.Xlibris.com
Orders@Xlibris.com

Norman "Spider" Weiss
USMA '46

It's Fun Being a Weiss Guy

Commercial Broker-Developer

From Failure to Success

In a world of saints and sinners—
I am no Saint

Florida to Florida
With one fascinating
Life in between

Contents

PREFACE

A True Story—as I could recollect it

The Army Colonel sitting in a chair across the desk from me unnerved me considerably. Why was I here? I was sixteen years old and a senior at Wyoming Seminary, a preparatory school for Methodist Ministers (Wesleyan was the college), and I had no idea as to what I was getting into. I had no thoughts of converting from my Jewish upbringing. It was winter in 1943. Thomas Byron Miller, our Congressman from Luzerne County, Pennsylvania, had been notified from the General Service Administration, to which he had assigned his privilege to appoint candidates to the Military Academy at West Point, that I was selected as one of two winners of the written contest that the GSA had conducted at Coughlin High School in Wilkes-Barre. This meant that I was to take a validating examination and a physical to see whether I was academically and physically fit.

I had not met Congressman Miller, but I had answered

his newspaper ad. His office secretary gave me a ticket to a competitive exam to be held at the Coughlin High School. When I saw Larry Miller (no relation to the Congressman) in the line waiting outside the high school to take the test, I guessed that I was hopelessly outclassed. I knew Larry, having played basketball against him. He was older and seemed physically better. My surprise at the Congressman's telephone statement was his further comment of congratulation that Larry Miller had also received an appointment. I learned later that alternates were appointed who all seemed to me to be better qualified. The locality in which we lived was Roman Catholic, and both Larry and I were Jewish. Why a prominent Catholic would appoint two Jewish boys was a mystery to me then and still is to this day.

I was notified to report to an Army office in a high-rise office building in New York City. I loved visiting New York but had no idea what I was to do there. I traveled up an elevator to a high floor and met an Army officer. He said he was a Colonel and wanted to know about my family background. I told him that I was born in 1926 in Daytona Beach, Florida, where my father was a real estate broker. My father had served in our Navy from 1916 to 1919 in the First World War. The Colonel said that he knew all he needed to know about my father, but he wanted further information about my mother. I was puzzled about this, but I had been told by my grandfather that he had served an eight-to-ten-year term in the Russian Army. The Colonel asked me if any other family members served in the Czarist Army. My grandfather had mentioned that he had a cousin about the same age. They were picked up by Cossacks while they were playing in the streets of their village near Kiev and were both inducted into the Russian Army. My grandfather was honorably discharged in 1902. He moved to Odessa since he thought he might find employment there. He corresponded with his cousin who had stayed in the army.

The Colonel then asked me if I spoke Russian. I did know a few swear words I had learned but did not speak the language. The Colonel then told me that my grandfather had a twin sister who had moved to Amsterdam. She was expected to immigrate to the United States in 1942. He did not know if she made it. His next comment left me speechless. Your grandfather's cousin was sent to the eastern part of Siberia where he was involved in a mutiny against his officers who were killed by their soldiers. The unit became bandits who lived off the land. My grandfather's cousin was the leader of one group, which fought against the Czarist regime and was embraced by the Communists. He became an officer in the Communist Army, which ended up in control of the country. He was, at that moment, in line to become part of the Russian Army's Chiefs of Staff and did end up there.

I guessed that was the reason I was accepted to our Military Academy. After all, we were allies of Russia in that war. It was probably the reason I was assigned to learn Russian at West Point when I had requested French.

This hour spent with the Colonel shaped my later life. It was a platform from which I made decisions later in life—powerful news for a sixteen-year-old. It gave me a reason to keep notes so that I could write about what happened later. The notes were destroyed in 1972; Hurricane Agnes was the culprit. It cost me a lot more than money and possessions. My story cannot be called biographical since I have, at age eighty-five, lost details of the stories which I'll now tell you. Even some of the names of the people I dealt with are not necessarily correct. I had an interesting and enjoyable life, learned some things which were not generally known. The details may have been altered, but the stories are all true.

My purpose in writing this memoir is to point out to you that the United States is far from a perfect country. To paraphrase Winston Churchill's comment on democracy being the worst form of government until you compare it to all others, I found it the country with the most problems, and my generation has moved to remedy them, but we are far from resolving them. Our worst problem—which may never be solved—is in electing people to govern us on the basis of popularity instead of genuine intelligent leadership. Elected officials in some areas are voted into office while still serving jail terms. Worse, some of our best generals are our worst enemies. We are human and, therefore, not perfect—but we are trying. Progress is being made.

Norm "Spider" Weiss (2011)

CHAPTER 1

Why I Was Motivated

I am among the last descendants of Abe Koff's grandchildren. My name is Norman Emanuel Weiss. I am the only descendant of Menachem Mendel Weiss to have been given his name. He was a tailor who had three wives in the course of a relatively short life in the village of Mihalovce, Slovakia. When my father, Aaron Weiss, was born there in 1894, he was the eighteenth child of his mother whose family name was Schwartz. She had lost four children in a row to her first husband, from whom she was divorced; none to her second, whose name was Feurman; and probably none to the Weisses, her third. All of her immediate family migrated to America—the Feurmans first and the Weisses last in 1906.

There were many cousins who lived in and around Mihalovce, and some who prospered in the neighboring countryside in the hotel business. They eventually moved to Budapest. All were slaughtered by the German Army (not the SS) in 1944 at the request of the Hungarian Nazi Party. Many of them had visited us when we lived on Terrace Street in Wilkes-Barre in 1933, but they had returned to Europe to take care of their extensive hotel holdings. Wilkes-Barre reminded them that they had a better life in Austria-Hungary, so they did not stay there. My father's entreaties to leave their children with us were ignored.

Because my life was so varied, I have divided it into chapters. There will be some overlapping since I have no notes or diaries. They were lost in the Susquehanna flood of June 1972. I am recollecting names and dates. However, all incidents are true. If you disagree with me on any matter, please bring your thoughts to my attention. My email address is weissdev@aol.com.

I cannot compete with master writers like Dan Brown who probably holds the title as one of the World's best fiction writers based on total circulation of his works. Or with Halberstam's *The Coldest Winter*, which accurately documented Korea. I have written this book to record some of my observations of many people with whom I have had contact. In the following series of stories—all of them true—you should understand why. My life was full of newsworthy contacts which very few people ever enjoy. Also, I was very lucky. My father advised me to be lucky rather than smart. I was.

I cannot present you with my autobiography for two reasons. The first is that the diary my mother insisted I keep was destroyed in the Wilkes-Barre flood in 1972 called Agnes, along with most of my official papers. The second is for an interesting one-day education session on what lawyers are allowed to publish. Having had a top-secret designation for a short period in the Army, I cannot speak or write about that. Nor can any lawyer reveal what a client has told him when seeking advice or preparing for litigation. However, I hope to amuse you with memoirs of many incidents in my life.

My father also advised me, after I told him that I was going to try an Army career, of an old Chinese blessing, which probably came out of a fortune cookie: "You should have a very interesting life." It was meant to be a curse. He was almost right. Since you are the reader, you can make a judgment.

I never had anything of importance to publish before except a magazine article, which I'll mention in Chapter 8. We took a psychological test after West Point graduation to establish what career we would prefer after Army service. It left me with two options: law and writing. The answers were surprising to me then. Not now. Following are the book's chapters. You can skip around the stories if you like. I have, to some extent.

This story is dedicated to my oldest son, Jim Weiss, who passed away unexpectedly on June 27, 2010, from an exploded aortic artery after having been admitted to a Johns Hopkins Hospital branch in Bethesda, Maryland. He was sixty years young at the peak of an outstanding law career in both our government's Justice Department and as a senior partner in the firm of Kirkpatrick, Lockhart, and Gates—one of the largest and most prestigious law firms in the United States. His clients were major New York Stock Exchange firms, and he traveled to many countries setting up offices and helping them to create antitrust laws which were new to them. He had asked me to write this book before he died. He seemed to have had a premonition of early death. He held a large dinner party for his wife's sixtieth birthday about four months early, explaining to me that he might not be around to have it at the time of her birthday. I thought nothing of it at the time since I knew that he was forced to travel all over the world in his branch of the legal profession. He was an unusually wonderful kid. My wife had passed away five years earlier, and this came as a double tragedy in a life that I never expected would last till now.

He left behind a loving widow, two children, and two

grandchildren. His funeral was the largest I ever attended. It was held in the funeral parlor belonging to one of his clients: Service Industries.

As author of this book, I used my nickname at West Point. It was earned when I was in beast barracks and subject to hazing by an anti-Semitic upperclassman who swore that he would have me thrown out because of my religion. My parents visited me and were shocked at my physical condition. I had an uncle, Jimmy Koff, who had married a lady whose family had a general store which had food. He sent me canned food, which I stored in my locker in the basement and visited at early hours to eat. I had enough body hair so that when classmates saw me in the "sinks" with my skinny frame, they compared me to "Spiderman"—a popular cartoon character at that time. I survived. Barely.

CHAPTER 2

Introduction

Growing Up in Wilkes-Barre and Kingston, Pennsylvania

My stay in Florida did not last long. My father's failure to anticipate the great '25 collapse in the real estate market prices caused him to send back all of the investors' money, if they wished. Most, but not all, wanted out. The investors who stayed in had properties transferred to them. By 1926, a recovery had started. But in April, the worst hurricane in Florida's history occurred, and all of his model homes were badly damaged along with his beachfront lots. These lots were turned over to the lender, which had financed his share of the Ormond Beach project. The bank later sold the individual lots originally costing about $30,000 each for $600 each. The storm had moved the beach to the west, shortening them considerably. Today, the lots should bring in this market $1,000,000 each since the beach has gradually been restored by government action. I do not know whether Rockefeller sold his. It's hard to say since he operated in multiple company names. The only income my father had was a meager one from a shoe store run by Jack Raub in Plymouth, a suburb of Wilkes-Barre. My mother called to see if she could get her teaching job back and was told that she could. They decided to move to Luzerne County in Northeast Pennsylvania, and did so quickly.

The first house we lived in was near the south end of South Franklin Street in Wilkes-Barre, which was an attached townhouse with small rooms. I was big enough to reach a wall from my crib, and promptly scribbled on it with crayons much color. The landlord's building inspector insisted that my father have the walls repainted. He could not afford to. We moved to the second floor of a house on the corner of Academy Street across from St. Peter's Church. I was still locked up in a crib there but alert enough to watch my mother use her cigarette lighter and smoke. I figured out how to reach through the walls of the crib, found the lighter, and proceeded to light a window curtain nearby. Fortunately, my mother was in our yard with the downstairs tenant who noticed the flaming curtain in the window. Sam Bellsey was a successful haberdasher. He was our neighbor downstairs. He knew workmen who repaired the damage. The landlord was not happy and suggested that we move again. We remained in the house for three more years since we had a lease. I started to grow up in that house and liked the neighbors who had children my own age. We did all sorts of mischievous things like capturing a tough tomcat, putting it in a burlap sack from the dump a block away, and depositing it in the mailbox used by the postman to collect the mail. We waited for what seemed like a long time to us for him to appear. The cat had come out of the bag and jumped on the mailman. We laughed hysterically. We had a neighbor a half block away who had a girl child who wanted to befriend us. We said fine, but since she was a girl, we had to paint her to look like a boy. She agreed; we used oil-based green paint to do the job. We never saw her again.

Our next house was at 58 Terrace Street in Wilkes-Barre. My father had accumulated enough money for the down payment on it. It had a nice yard with a toolhouse made of dry old wood. My mother liked to entertain her friends in the yard. She set up a card table near the house and was playing cards there on an afternoon. She had put marshmallows on the kitchen counter. I convinced Bobby Reiser next door to help toast them because I had seen my mother do this. We gathered twigs and newspaper and made a fire on the wooden floor of the toolshed and hid it from the bridge-playing ladies. My brother Herbie came over since he had seen me take the marshmallows and he wanted some. We told him that if he could bring enough water out from the kitchen to put out the fire, which was burning through the floor, we would give him some. He ran back and forth while we tried to stamp out the fire. I thought that if we opened the door, the smoke would leave and the fire would go out. To the contrary, it got worse, and the roof started to burn. Herbie went to the table to complain that I wouldn't give him any marshmallows because they were all burned up. The ladies were astounded to see the flames coming out, and one went into the house to call the fire department. The fire truck arrived in a few minutes and extinguished the blaze. I had gone next door to the Reiser house to hide in their basement.

When I came home, my mother said nothing. My father was fortunately out of town. The next day, she drove me out to the county juvenile prison, Kislyn. I had to remove my shoes before entering. When we went inside, I was surprised to see two of my neighborhood friends, Junee and Mark. I asked Mark how he liked it there. He said that the food wasn't too bad—better than home—but he hated not having his shoes. He said that he was stuck there because he couldn't walk over the crushed rock with its sharp edges without them. On the way home, my mother told me that she was one of the Directors of Kislyn and could arrange for my admission there if I had another fire. I never did.

Wilkes-Barre was probably the best town in the United States for a Jewish kid in which to grow up. It was, after the Susquehanna Indians were all converted to Christianity and died out, turned into a predominantly Welsh community. The coal mines had been discovered. There were not enough Welsh immigrants to keep up with the substantial requirement for miners. The next waves of immigrants were Irish and Polish.

The ethnic groups which arrived later settled for the most part into their own enclaves. The demand for coal became great. The mine owners controlled the lives of the mine workers through ownership of the majority of housing units. The company stores provided all things necessary for survival and profits for the owners. Miners who had families had adequate pay, but not enough to live comfortable lives. The wives, in many instances, moved to New York or Philadelphia. The owners induced female workers to work in local sewing plants to augment miners' income. It helped, but the mine owners' families also did not want to live there. Miners were paid in coupons only exchangeable in company stores. Laws were passed requiring pay to be in dollars. The mine stores went out of business.

Each ethnic group had its own churches, and there were many of them. The heads of the churches had a meeting in the 1850s and decided that it would be in the town's benefit to improve it by bringing in Jewish immigrants. After all, they were merchants so that the ladies would stay. This was not unusual in those days. It happened all over the country. The Goldwaters in Arizona are an example. The Jewish immigrants were not coming since there was no synagogue in the town. The churches provided enough money to build a synagogue, and Temple B'nai Brith was born. It exists to this day, although in another location. The idea worked, and many immigrants came in—mostly from New York City, which had open battles between the Italians and the Irish in the streets. Even a prominent Jewish lawyer moved in. He became a judge shortly and was taken into the Westmoreland Club, which was an outgrowth of the church next door's men's club.

Most of the first Jewish families who moved into the area were from Germany, settling along the banks of the Susquehanna River. The residents who became affluent were familiar with the not-infrequent flooding and had moved farther inland. Terrace Street was just one block away from the river. It was a completely different world to me. Since my family was not German and now well above the poverty line, my father looked for another location of which there were plenty available in 1936.

I had a very pleasant few years on Terrace Street and did not want to move to Kingston since I had no friends there. Once I owned a bicycle, it was easy for me to get around town. Our immediate neighborhood had families which were closely knit. The Klein family lived on West Academy Street, and my future wife lived there along with her older brother Howard who was an excellent athlete. Anna Newman Klein and my mother were schoolmates and decided to have their children born at the same time so that they would continue a family relationship when they reached marital age.

On a trip to Europe in 2008, I detoured a day to spend in that town, Mihalovce. I had rented a car and driver for the day. The town had been selected by Stalin as an ideal place to develop a communist government. He had the town redeveloped in a modern way with the demolition of the center of the town (which had grown into a city), with two large hotels, many apartment and commercial buildings, and a large shopping center in the middle of it. The old Count's castle and the one Jewish graveyard had stones dating back to the expulsion of Jews from Spain. The old Jewish section was gone, along with the synagogue. The graveyard was intact, but overgrown with heavy grass and weeds. My guide told me that the graveyard had been abandoned after the Second World War. The oldest graves dated back to the 1400s. My grandfather, Menachem Mendel Weiss, was buried there in 1905. The gravestones were all identical and extremely difficult to read. I looked for but could not locate a Weiss or Fierman anywhere.

The population came from Northern Spain, having been chased out by the royalty since Jews were not allowed to remain there unless converted to Christianity. The castle in town, which although built in several different periods, had many of the same features of 46 East Dorrance Street, Kingston, Pennsylvania, and probably was the reason that my father liked the property he bought from Anne Dorrance in 1938. The nearby village where the Weiss Inn, run by his uncle, that my father visited, has disappeared. The family, many of whom visited us when we lived in Wilkes-Barre, had moved to Budapest where they all perished. This trip caused one of my saddest days.

Jerry Fierman's twin sister Shirley, known as "Aunt Gorgeous," lives in the Pennsylvania community. Her twin brother Jerry has predeceased her. He had visited Mihalovce a year ahead of me and also tried to find relatives. Josh Noble, grandson of Louie Noble, an Auschwitz survivor, graduated from West Point and is now a member of the Army Reserve. He is becoming a Rabbi to enter the Chaplain's Corps. The range of studies allowed at West Point now is unbelievable.

Many members of the Jewish Community in Wilkes-Barre were involved in the Jewish Community Center. My membership in AZA (a junior branch of B'nai Brith) was looked upon favorably when I had applied for admission to West Point, and when I moved back to Wilkes-Barre, I was its adult director for several years. The population of Wilkes-Barre included blacks. Not all of them came to town with the Underground Railroad as runaway slaves. Some of them became good businessmen. Olin Morris ran a popular local jewelry store and was at one time President of our local Rotary Club. Many of my schoolmates when living on Terrace Street were black. My house in Kingston was not far from Terrace Street, and I used my bicycle to stay in contact with my friends for years after we moved.

The house my dad wanted was not for sale. It was the new Dorrance home that had been built after the original 1787 one burned in 1927. By 1929, the new house was up and ready. The Dorrance sisters who planned to live in it could not afford to do so since they had other residences and not enough money to support the staff the house required. They rented it to a Weiss family to whom we were not related. These Weisses were apparently from the New York area and were in the bootlegging business. They were caught, and one went to jail. The house became available. Anne Dorrance still refused to sell but rented it to my father. He pulled down interior false walls which had been erected to hide the liquor stock—a small amount of which was still there. Because my dad was not able to purchase the house, he purchased another a few blocks away and told our landlady that we would move there at our lease expiration two years away. Anne Dorrance could not rent the house for enough money to cover the operating costs. She agreed to a sale. My father paid her $10,000 more than her asking price. She needed the money, and he recognized that. He did that more than once in his real estate transactions. I questioned him about that a number of years later. He replied that being in the real estate business he learned that commercial property was only worth what the property would return in the future. Residential property was different. Colonel Dorrance had been granted that property after the Revolution with that location as payment for his contribution to the war of liberation from England. He had raised a regiment in Philadelphia, paid his troops out of his own funds, and had not been reimbursed. He organized a group of fellow officers in the same circumstances, and went with them to President Washington's office in Philadelphia. With drawn swords, they threatened to kill him unless he turned over to them the equivalent amounts of gold or land which he had available. A painting of this action is in the library of Winterthur, a former DuPont residence. (Upon a visit to this library, I was struck by the resemblance of the room to the library of the house I was raised in from age nine to seventeen. I discovered that the architect was the same one for both houses. My father said that he knew that the price was well below market, and he did not want to appear to be taking advantage of the depression real estate market. He was that way all his life).

The move to Kingston from Wilkes-Barre in February of 1936 was fortuitous. The Susquehanna went through its ritual of flooding the area during April rains. The flood had damaged the house on Terrace Street, but the water did not rise to the level of the house in Kingston into which twelve families plus ours moved. I moved out to stay with my Uncle Jim over Levinson's general grocery and hardware store in Larksville. My room on Dorrance Street was necessary for the guests. Our Kingston house had received no flooding until 1972 when river dikes gave way and left eighty thousand people in the Valley homeless. The house I built at the rear of the Dorrance Street one had five feet of water on the ground floor and could not be occupied for five months.

Changing schools in midterm was difficult for me. Thanks to my mother, I was prepared to handle fights, which normally occurred in my life whenever we moved. However, in Kingston a few days after we moved, I was attacked by a threesome—the fat one of which pulled me down from the rear of my shoulders to the ground while the other two beat me while screaming with large sticks in the groin area leaving a bloody mess. The threesomes were institutionalized later since they were mentally ill and were confined to a state institution for defective children. I thought that the screaming one was a witch. I believed in witches in those days. My visit to Dr. Dattner, our physician, was discouraging. He told me that the testicles—which, fortunately, had not yet dropped—were damaged, and I might not be able to use them. I had no idea what he was talking about. He was wrong. The testicles were not damaged permanently, and fortunately, had no effect on my later life.

Kingston schooling was from the fifth grade through the eighth grade at the public schools two blocks from my house. My mother insisted that I go to high school at Wyoming Seminary, a private prep school, which was founded to create Methodist Ministers who would complete their training at Wesleyan College in Connecticut. My father wanted me to attend the Hill School in Pottstown instead. He had been raised in Pottstown. I was not in favor of either, but Wyoming Seminary was one mile close to home (not one hundred miles away), and I could socialize with the friends I had made in public schools. Wyoming Seminary was just right for me. After four years of Bible studies, and daily chapel attendance, I had a very good idea about religion. I discovered that the Methodist training was to my mind almost the same as Hebrew school training except for the acceptance of Jesus as God and the fact that we studied in English whereas Hebrew school training was in Hebrew, which I never learned to speak or understand. Other than that I had no problems regarding religion. I was quite lucky at school. I contributed articles to our school newspaper, was elected to the editorship of our class annual, and was also elected to be captain of the tennis team and manager of the football team. In the class poll at the end of our senior year I was elected "Most Likely to Succeed" and "Best Dressed." In the competition for the best speaker in the debate held during the senior year, I was elected the winner and awarded a $25 prize, the first and largest I had ever received. My father told me to give it back to the school, which I did. I played basketball well enough for the second team—not the first. I was active on the swim team but never won in a meet. All these accolades helped me, I am sure, to get into a decent college. However, with the war fever on, I really wanted to go to either Annapolis or West Point. It happened. I had applied to all military programs available, but was not accepted at any of them.

I graduated with honors and entered West Point on July 1, 1943. I was among the youngest members of my class. It might have been a mistake to take up a military career for the next ten-plus years. The day I entered, I thought I had achieved the best success of my life. It took only twenty-four hours to change my mind.

Psychologically, I was ill prepared for West Point. With all the honors I had achieved in prep school, I was not ready for the reception which I received. I expected that I would probably have to fight my way into being accepted. This had happened to me previously in public schools, and West Point was a public school. I had no idea that the institution was racist. I thought that most of the students were political pets and there because of political connections. This was wartime. None of the cadets I met had appointments by winning a publicly open GSA-controlled contest. After the openly racist reception, I wanted to leave immediately. I felt that I should talk to my parents about it first. I expected that to remain at the Academy would be years of misery, and I had no idea as to how I could possibly fit in. Apparently, I was not the only one I met who felt that way. There were a number of resignations. One fellow plebe resigned and showed up in our company two years later with captain bars. He had been accepted into an officer's candidate school and had been shipped overseas in an infantry unit which saw some action and had battlefield promotions. We were jealous.

Entering West Point cadets
Norm Weiss, Jack Mangan, Larry Miller

CHAPTER 3

College

US Military Academy at West Point

On July 1, 1943, I entered West Point. I attended a lecture in a large hall. There were over 1,300 new entering cadets present. The speaker was an officer. I didn't know whether he was the Commandant or the Superintendent. I had never been there before. He reminded us that we were at war and would only attend three years instead of the normal four. We would receive all of the necessary academics and training in that abbreviated session. He also said to look to the right and left of you. One of the two will not graduate since we have a grading system based on where you stand in your class. You will be placed in a company depending on your height. We went from there to the cadet store where we were measured and issued uniforms and new shoes. We were told to take care of our clothes since the cost of them would come out of our pay. I was delighted to hear that we were getting paid to go to college. So was my father, I'm sure.

We were lined up in the southern paved area of the dormitories by height and separated into companies. I found myself assigned to G-2 Company and, at 6'1", was the shortest cadet in it. We stood in the square and listened to the Corps' first captain. He gave us a speech telling us that we are now in "Beast Barracks" and, as such, must obey certain stringent rules as part of our initiation and training. There were certain rules that turned me off completely; one was that we had to obey all commands of our cadet overseer regardless of whether we thought they were proper. If we became enraged at the overseer and hit him, we would be assigned a placc in the gym where we could fight. If I won the match, I had to fight every member in his class until physically beaten to a point where I was unable to fight further. I thought that my boxing training would help in the first fight, but I did not see how I could ultimately win. I followed my mother's advice to fight when you think you can win, but if you think you will lose, don't fight at all. It seemed to me that I couldn't possibly win under these conditions. The other statement the Cadet First Captain made was that there was a "nigger" in the cadet ranks that did not fit into our Army since the Army was segregated. No one in the class was allowed to talk to him as he was "silenced." I felt as if I had been kicked in the stomach at this. I had gone to grade school with blacks and never had given a thought to segregation. The black cadet's name was McCoy, and he was assigned to H-2, the company next to me. On a break, I looked at the cadets in H-2 and could not pick him out. I was told he was from Philadelphia or Pittsburgh. I felt a strong urge to volunteer to live with him. However, I figured with being Jewish, and if silenced with this guy, I would never graduate. I did not see him then or later. He must have been kept isolated since my company quarters were near to H-2 and he was never visible to me.

When I went back to the temporary quarters to which I had been assigned, I met my cadet overseer. His name was George Doud. He introduced himself by saying that he disapproved of Jews coming into the Academy and that he would have me expelled within the plebe year. I told him that the first class at West Point was 50 percent Jewish. He did not bother to answer that but said that since I talked back he was awarding me my first demerit. Also, I would stand at attention all night in the hallway and he would check on me periodically. I stood at attention all night dozing on my feet when my classmates said that he wasn't around. The next day we were assigned to tables in the mess hall. My table commander was Doud. He ordered me to sit under the table and told my classmates that they were forbidden to give me any food. That particular form of torture was not uncommon. The cadets at every table were required to eat a "square" meal. This was not only annoying but cut down on the amount of food they could enjoy. One section of the dining area was set aside for the football team. There was no torture there. Their menu was a great deal different from the regular mess. This business of having no food was a standard operation for Doud who was a turn-back—a cadet who had failed his first year and was allowed back upon completion of make-up courses. He probably felt that he would pick up extra points on his evaluation of grade average by forcing new cadets to either resign or get so many demerits that they would be dropped from the rolls. This treatment continued for the next few weeks.

I lost a good deal of weight so that my clothes did not fit properly. I was anything but an ideal-looking cadet. I was forced to spend all my free time walking punishment tours on the area located between the buildings on the campus center. Fortunately, I had some help from my classmates in the dining room who would surreptitiously hand me food under the table. I was able to put butter passed to me on the soles of Doud's shoes. Contact with the smooth floor kept him unbalanced. I had so many demerits assigned that I spent over a hundred hours on the area.

Most of the demerits came from Doud, of course, but during inspections from other cadet officers, I looked a mess with big clothes and sloppy.

Life at West Point wasn't all nightmares. I had two interesting roommates: Jack Matteson, an army brat, and Rocco Petrone, an ice dealer's son from Albany, New York. We were all very different from one another but strengthening in a way. Rocco had been a football player in Albany and immediately was put on our team, which was certainly the best college team at that time. Earl Blake was a West Point graduate coach who Rocco thoroughly disliked. However, Blake put together a stunning combination of Blanchard, Davis, Tucker, and Pool, and never lost a game. Rocco said that when he first went out to practice, the team had elected a captain who normally decides the direction of play at the start of the game. There was one black cadet who appeared to be a highly desirable player during practice sessions. Blake told the team captain that no "nigger" was going to play on any of his teams. The team captain resigned on the spot. Blake told him to suit up before every game and take the coin toss. Then he was to proceed to the bench to sit out every game. Rocco, in disgust, decided that he did not want to be part of that team and played sloppily so that he was shifted to the second team, which played secondary schools. He had the courage of his convictions, and I admired him for it. He, fortunately, had a brilliant mathematical mind and stood high in the class averages. We occasionally had battalion lectures by outstanding speakers. One was Albert Einstein from Princeton. Einstein gave our class his lecture on relativity. It was so complicated to my mind that I left the lecture at a point where I could not understand it. He spoke with a strong German accent and used a cadet to put his diagrams on the blackboard. Rocco stayed to the end and later explained it to Jack and me in our room. He went into Ordinance but joined NASA after graduation. He became the Chief Flight Controller in Apollo 13, which gave him national recognition on television. He also worked with Von Braun to make our planes safer and develop rockets enabling us to reach the moon. Von Braun stated that he was a valuable member of his team.

Jack Matteson elected to be in the infantry during his postgraduate career. He was one of the first officers to be sent by President Johnson to train the South Vietnamese Army and among the last to leave Vietnam when our forces were required to close up shop there. When I visited Jack at his home in Carmel, which his father had built not too far from Clint Eastwood's place, he had a large wall picture frame with dozens of medals and occupation ribbons on it. One was the Vietnam Medal of Honor. Jack had borrowed, without permission, an Army helicopter and used it for battle observation. He had thought of resigning when ordered by his commanding officer, General Westmoreland, to issue artificial body counts of killed North Vietnamese soldiers. He said that it cost him his recommendation for a star (Brigadier General) rank. When I asked him why he did not obey orders, he thought, and said he remembered Rocco's story about Blake and refused orders he felt were wrong. West Point is ingrained in him. He retired as a Colonel. He never came back for a reunion. I did not mention to him that our Honor Code allows lies for military purposes.

After more than one month of Beast Barracks we were trucked to Pine Camp, near Watertown, New York, for tank training under the command of General Oliver who had been transferred from North Africa. The training was excellent and I loved every minute of it except when the sergeant teaching me how to run the tank, fire the guns accurately, and move quickly to another hull defilade position suggested that I try some of his chewing tobacco. I had never done that before. It was distress when I was not allowed to use any tank opening to spit out the tobacco. He said that we were operating under combat training conditions and no openings were allowed. When I asked him what to do with it, he suggested swallowing it. I got sick. It caused him to make the comment that I would never use chewing tobacco in a tank again and that might save my life some day. A tough lesson, but an unforgettable one.

When we returned to West Point, the atmosphere was different. I still had a lot of demerits to walk off, but received fewer than normal. I had been assigned to take Russian as a language along with a few of my classmates. I developed my first feelings that I was in no way in control of my life. However, at age seventeen, I really did not expect to be. My weight had come up to 130 lbs., and it was a definite improvement. My academic grades were quite satisfactory, especially in mathematics. Wyoming Seminary's college preparation was excellent. I was assigned as a tutor to a cadet from E-1 Company who was a turn-back and had been deficient in math. His name was Bernie Janis. He turned out to be one of my best lifelong friends. I was best man at his wedding, and he was best man at my second one in Florida. Bernie was a slow thinker, but to my mind quite bright. Our academic classes were set up with fifteen students in each. We faced the blackboards around the room and wrote the answers to problems presented to us by the teacher who usually was an Army officer. Each question had a short time in which to respond. Bernie's thinking process was thorough but not quick enough so that he frequently left the board vacant. I reported this, and he transferred to a class where the questioning was slower. He did so well there that we had free time when together and played tennis. Bernie used his polo pony, which was allowed at the Academy at that time, and played on our polo team. That allowed him extra time off and a seat at the team tables in the Mess Hall. He thoroughly enjoyed being at West Point, having spent his entire preliminary education from six years old at a military academy.

We were lucky to be allowed to leave the grounds on occasional weekends. Now cadets have much fewer restrictions as far as attendance is concerned. Even the dress has changed to where the stiff collars worn with the uniforms are not regularly required. At a reunion a few years back, I decided to look up a cadet that I had recommended to my Congressman for an appointment and who was now matriculating at the institution. I found his room in complete disarray. We had daily inspections to preclude this lack of housekeeping, I was told that inspections did occur but on an irregular basis.

The campus has changed to the extent that the school looks like a college campus instead of the military post it once was. This is due to the great increase in cadet numbers and the necessity of adding structures to accommodate it. The parades are not as they were since the companies no longer have uniform heights and have women and blacks mixed in with the cadets. The cadet population is highly selective to this day. The cadets have much more freedom to choose their subjects and plans for the future after graduation. Whether or not this will increase or decrease the strength of the military is still uncertain. It sure would have helped me both psychologically and physically. The almost religious worship of sports has disappeared for the most part. Sports are greeted in a more realistic way. Congress is not happy about the academic scandals which have occurred in the past and the Academy administrators are still using the strict Honor Code as part of the educational system.

At graduation, I was ecstatic that I was released from what I considered the equivalent of a jail term. I had received a good education and had a decent job in front of me. I had no sterling record of achievement but I had more than recovered from the way

I was on entrance. I weighed 160 lbs., mostly of muscle developed in the gymnasium. I was in the top third of the class physically and mentally. I had been knocked out with broken ribs of the one sport for which I qualified, Lacrosse, but ran cross-country to build up my stamina. When I took Branch Immaterial Training at Fort Benning, our first assignment after being commissioned, I had reached age twenty and had no problem breezing through the course. The Academy had totally turned my life around. I was grateful to it despite all. Today's institution is much different and infinitely better. I am sure that I would enjoy the training now in contrast to what I went through then.

1943 was the war year in which the Russians defeated the Germans at Stalingrad. It was questionable as to how much time would elapse until the end of hostilities. In an average class, 40 percent of the graduates leave the service quickly. Field-grade officers hang on until they can make a business contact or retire at the highest rank they can get. Not generally known, but true nonetheless, is that the Army cannot promote you above the rank of Colonel. The Military Affairs Committee of Congress promotes all of our generals, even over the military's objections. Admiral Hyman Rickover is a typical example. Because of that, you are always respectful of Congressmen—particularly the ones from your own state.

As a new cadet, I had been placed in a company depending on my height, which was 6'1". I was skinny at 145 lbs., but fairly agile since I had engaged in sports activities at Wyoming Seminary. I could never forget the first day. The Army was segregated into black and white units. In the section of Pennsylvania in which I was raised, blacks may have been second-class citizens, but they were accepted—particularly on the sports teams—as equals. West Point was not a private school.

My parents visited me after the first two weeks. We had lunch at the Hotel Thayer. Pictures taken by my sister Nancy at that time showed me as a rumpled uniform sorry cadet. My mother stated that not liking the food was no excuse not to eat it. She had no idea of what the hazing was.

Other problems were overcome one at a time. I never grew to like the Academy even after a poor plebe year. I never even tried to look the part of a spruced up cadet. I became an "area bird" because I figured that with enough demerits, I could get expelled. The academics were not at all difficult, and I enjoyed the company of my two roommates. I was called up before an officer disciplinary board because of my record of demerits, but it was later in my first-class year, so they let me stay even though I did not request it. I was surprised to receive sergeant's stripes for my uniform. Unfortunately, they were taken away before graduation because of a minor violation of discipline. I graduated bare sleeved.

Life at the military academy after an extremely difficult plebe year had its good moments. I had been accepted to play lacrosse. I had two ribs broken in my first game and was disqualified for the season. It also allowed me a respite from walking punishment tours on the asphalt area slabs, and I began to put back my lost weight and gain some strength. My plebe summer was partially spent at Pine Camp, New York, near Watertown.

When we returned to West Point we started our academic season. The difficulties of Beast Barracks had toned down considerably. I did well academically but continued to pick up demerits from the same upperclassman who swore that he would force me out. I was permitted to choose a foreign language. Having had three years of French at Wyoming Seminary, I naturally chose that. I had been surprised to be assigned to Russian. I guess it was because my grandfather had been in the Russian Army. The language I learned came in very handy when

I finally got to meet Russians in Europe. The basic courses were not difficult, and I was ahead of the class because of having a Wyoming Seminary education. I had some free time even with the punishment tours. Bernie Janis was looking for a tennis partner, and we played quite a few times. That was fortuitous since we became great friends and remained so until he died May 1, 2010. I gave the eulogy at his funeral.

During sophomore year, the class schedule became much tougher since the four years had been trimmed to three years, and extra subjects had to be inserted into our schedule. I had become used to the study system whereby you were expected to learn the subject from the textbooks provided. In the classrooms of about fifteen students each, you stood facing a blackboard while the teacher would have you write answers to the questions he asked. You were graded daily during this session, and your class standing based on these grades was posted on a bulletin board for all to see. We were constantly reminded that one-third of the entering class would not graduate, so you did not want to be anywhere near the bottom. A few resignations and one apparent suicide occurred during our plebe year because of these pressures. Yearling year was not easier for all concerned.

The summer after yearling year, we were stationed at summer camp then known as Camp Popolopen—now called Camp Buckner. I was friendly with a classmate who was quite a bit older since he had gone to Penn State before coming to West Point. We had the privilege of inviting young ladies to our weekend hops, which were far less formal than the ones during the academic year. His name was Marty Cutler, and he was from Shenandoah, Pennsylvania. He suggested that we invite two girls to a dance, and he had an idea as to how to get them. We had passed a girls' camp on one of our fieldtrips, which was only a few miles away from our quarters. We didn't know its name, but we observed that it was a girls' camp.

Marty told me that two girls from the camp we had secretly visited on the outside were coming to the weekend hop. We had left the camp we were living in and hitched a ride to the girls' camp. We stayed outside their camp until we picked up the names of two girls. We were able to return to our cabins without being detected. He had their names, and we could meet them at the cadet hostess's desk. When I went to the lady chaperone to meet my unknown date, she turned livid with rage. She told me that I had done something for which she was sure I would be severely punished. I responded with a request to at least meet one of the girls so I could determine whether she was worth the punishment she promised I would have. That only caused her to become more inflamed than ever. I never got to meet them. I felt sorrier for them than for us. The chaperone had assigned two cadets to take care of them, and we left the hop. I told Marty that I hoped they enjoyed themselves.

The hop was at the end of summer activities, and we moved back to our assigned quarters. About a week after our return, I was awakened at midnight by a night guard and told to report immediately to the Commandant's office. I dressed quickly and headed on Diagonal Walk to the office. I suspected that it was because of the hostess's furor. Night meetings were held for honor violations, and I wondered what code section I might have violated. Our cadet company captain was present along with the Commandant and the Army officer in charge of our company. An honor roll member was also there. My nerves were on edge, but I knew that I had to stay steady since whatever I was charged with was a dismissible offense.

The questioning was about how and why we left camp. I was blunt in stating that I never committed an honor violation and merely put into practice going out and in through enemy lines without being observed. One of the officers said that they had talked to Marty Cutler, and he had given them a report that I was with him. I confirmed that I was in full agreement with Marty's plan and that we had not been stopped going back so that there could not have been an honor violation. Not only that, but two exceptions to the Honor Code were lies for the purpose of Military Intelligence, and when it involved social activities with women. They appeared amused at my answers, told me not to talk to Marty again, and dismissed me. I felt much better going back on Diagonal Walk. Marty was not in my section of the Corps, and I rarely saw him anyway. I regarded this forced separation from a fellow I felt was a friend as a form of punishment. Marty graduated but was not commissioned at graduation because of physical reasons. He became a lawyer after leaving the service and died not too many years later from a bad heart condition. I felt that the Army would have had a good officer had he not had that condition.

Marty had figured that during the two hours that cadets were at the movie theater we could hitch a ride on the highway to the camp, get close enough to hear conversations and see what the girls looked like, get their names if possible, and call them up to invite them the next day. As evening fell, it became dark and we were able to get to the road unobserved. The plan worked since we were not discovered coming back except possibly by some of our classmates who were not on guard duty so that they had no obligation to turn us in.

First class year had Hundredth Night. That is one hundred days before graduation. You receive your class ring and have a big name dance band in celebration. I invited a young lady I had met at a previous dance to come up for the affair, and she accepted. About a week before Hundredth Night, she called me stating that she was in bed with pneumonia and could not come. On my regular Sunday call home, I mentioned the fact to my mother that I had lost my date to Hundredth Night. She suggested that I ask Zelda Klein, who she had decided I would marry when I was sixteen. I knew Zelda well, but she was two years behind me in school, and we had never dated. However, I called her at the University of Chicago, and she accepted—to my surprise.

Zelda was to arrive at the Hotel Thayer on Saturday morning of Hundredth Night. Friday, at the mess hall, the punishment for gambling was read. I had paid ten cents to a cadet who was selling a basketball pool where, if you guessed the total score, you won a prize. I had never done that before. I was company orderly at the time. I threw the purchased ticket away because I felt that the odds were too small and I did not want to be caught with anything that looked like gambling. Jesse Harris, a classmate who had dropped a water bag on me when I was stationed as an outside guard, was sitting in my room next to the orderly room taking a break. When I walked in, I told my two roommates that all was quiet. There was a cadet selling basketball pool tickets, but I got rid of him by buying a ticket and then throwing it away. Jesse Harris made his presence known, however, by calling from his chair, "You familiar with the fact that I'm on guard and I have to report all instances of gambling?" I was shocked and told him that I was buying peace and didn't even keep the ticket. He reported me anyway. As a result, I lost my sergeant stripes and was given punishment of being confined to quarters over the weekend.

This put me in a very difficult situation. Zelda was on her way from Chicago. She wasn't an ordinary date. We had never dated before, and when she arrived at West Point, I would not be allowed to see her. I could get her a substitute escort—it had happened to me once before—but the girl I had invited never spoke to me again. I felt that her family and mine would be aggravated over the circumstances. I had to get a postponement of the punishment. After dinner, I visited the Commandant's quarters to request this, but he had left the campus for the weekend. Looking to the right, I saw lights in the Superintendent's house. I knocked on the door and, luckily, the Academy Superintendent, General Maxwell Taylor, answered it himself. I hurriedly explained my dilemma before he could order me out and take my name for more demerits. He asked me to sit down and asked me questions about my date. When I told him that this was more than a date and families' sensibilities were involved, he asked me why I was receiving punishment. I told him what had happened. He sympathized with me but allowed me to start my tours on Monday morning. When I left, he said, "You know, I think you're going to marry this girl." I denied it, saying that this was my first date with her. General Taylor was a keen observer of personalities, I later discovered in Germany.

Zelda arrived, and I never told her what had happened. I believe that she enjoyed the weekend. I certainly did, and I did not remove my sergeant's stripes until after she left on Sunday evening. I'm not sure that she even noticed them, but I was concerned that if I removed the stripes, it would show on the uniform and explanations would have to occur.

There is no question that the Academy was beginning to change before I left it. No demerits and even some approvals from a few of the tactical officers. Colonel William McKinley was our company's officer for a short time. He told me that I would make an excellent officer if I set my sights on the moon. He commented that even if I fell short, I would have gone a long way up. He recommended me to have sergeant stripes on my sleeve, which I did wear for a time. Other officers were also helpful in building up my confidence. My academic grades were always good but rarely of star quality, and my military bearing and physical condition had improved substantially.

We had been allowed to take two-day weekends after the war ended, and I took advantage of it to visit my home in Kingston and make visits to Vassar not far north on the Hudson. On one of my hometown visits, a Colonel stopped by to offer my father a job as military commander in Budapest. I was present when he was in our home and mishandled a soda bottle so that the Colonel was splashed. My father turned down the offer, stating that he had no one he could rely on to continue his growth of his shoe chain stores. He also said that were he to be put in charge in Hungary, he did not feel that he could control his emotions to be able to govern efficiently. After all, every one of his family had been murdered by the German and Hungarian troops. The Colonel was surprised at this, but seemed to understand. I was surprised myself.

Friendships with fellow cadets were many, and although almost all of my close friends are not alive today, they added color and an appreciation of being in the military I never would have had otherwise.

CHAPTER 4

The Army and Life

The joy of having completed the three difficult years soon wore off. I was sent to Fort Benning to complete the ninety-day wonder course that all graduates receive and later to the Jeffersonville Depot where I learned a good deal about Graves Registration Service. The depot purchased the coffins in which our overseas dead were transported back to their homes for burial. What a first assignment! I could not figure out what breach of disciplinary rule set me up for that assignment, but I requested to be assigned to troop duty. That you could always get. I was sent to Camp Lee to command a black laundry service company just returned from Germany. I figured that I was destined to get the Army's worst assignments. I was right. The company commander was white. The rest of the company was 100 percent black. The captain left the same day I relieved him, but the first sergeant was a career soldier twice my age and very smart about Army ways. The company mission was to be dissolved, so that every day we became smaller. However, the assignment became very interesting when I had to bring back an arrested private requiring a hearing with Judge Shepherd.

My visit to Judge Shepherd's home had been interesting. I met both of his daughters, Crit and Dottie. They were pretty and just slightly younger. I invited both of them out for dinner in the officers' mess and gave one of my classmates the choice of either. He was, and should have been, delighted. My luck had finally changed. I needed that since Hundredth Night at West Point.

We were granted two months' leave to make up for the leave time we would have received during a normal school year without any. My father had bought a large house on the boardwalk in Atlantic City for use by his employees on their vacation time if they wished. I spent my time there painting and fixing it up. After that, I was ready for the Fort Benning Branch Immaterial Training.

Army life after West Point's graduation was genuinely interesting and satisfactory, particularly if you were allowed to pursue the activities your branch required. The war had ended with a surplus of unemployed soldiers, sailors, marines, and pilots. Few of us wanted to leave the Service which had set the minimum time for it at three years. Branches to serve in had to be selected before graduation. The services such as engineers, ordinance, signal corps, quartermaster corps, transportation corps, etc., were selected by cadets in the upper third of the class. Infantry invariably came in last for obvious reasons. I elected to go into the Quartermaster Corps after a discussion with my father who had wanted me to go into the Navy in the first place. He felt that I should have better experience to help me enter business at a higher level when I left the Army. My first choice had been Cavalry. I remembered my Pine Camp training days and the fascination I had with the giant machines, the tanks. Apparently, other cadets felt the same way so that I was not accepted in that branch even though I was lucky enough to be in the top third. Twenty-four of our class of 825 were allowed to become Quartermasters.

After our two months leave, the entire class less the hundred graduating fliers went to Fort Benning to take the Branch Immaterial Training that most ninety-day wonders received instead of training at West Point. It was relatively easy when compared to our previous training. As Quartermasters, we were treated for some reason as Infantrymen. We were running around the base while the Infantry was riding in buses—or so it seemed. After a few months of this type of action, we were sent to our basic service branch. I had sufficient time off to visit my cousin Bud Weiss who had married an Atlanta girl, and I was introduced to the Standard Club in that city. It was a different world from the Army and Wilkes-Barre. I did meet an eligible lady, but at age twenty, I was not ready for any commitment.

Previously mentioned, when I was transferred to Camp Lee in Virginia, my assignment was to take command of a Quartermaster Laundry Company which had just returned from Germany and was 100 percent black, except for the Captain who was white. I was happy since I had been assigned there during yearling year to train illiterate draftees how to march and become soldiers. I was not happy to be told that I would probably be put in the boat section since the Navy had lost too many ensigns who were piloting landing craft for landing in Italy in the face of shore bombardment and needed replacements. It was our first encounter with untrained troops. I had decided to visit Annapolis as an exchange student. I had met Jimmy Carter there. It convinced me not to join the Navy.

Eisenhower was not yet in a position to remove the stigma of a segregated military force. My time of training from the company's Captain who could not wait to be relieved was thirty minutes. I was lucky that the first sergeant was quite competent. The troops had been overseas and were, in some cases, not manageable. They were being discharged based on their service time, which in most cases was sufficient to allow honorable discharges.

Eisenhower decided to make changes in the Army that should have been made years before. The pressures of finishing the war delayed curing obvious problems. One of the principal changes was officers' uniforms. We had to look like enlisted men—with shinier shoes, of course. All junior officers who were involved with troops were required to attend a two week course which taught you not only how to cook but also show you what an Army kitchen should look and act like. I liked the first week of classroom training but found the second one in the kitchen difficult. I had a company to run.

Commanding my first company meant that I had to stop in the orderly room every morning and evening to take care of the administrative affairs. On my second day of cooking classes, before I reported to the class, the first sergeant handed me an order from the local magistrate's office in Hopewell to appear in his courtroom at 10:00 a.m. to defend one of our company's soldiers who had been arrested and was being held in jail. The sergeant said that he had issued him an overnight pass and was surprised when he did not show up for duty that morning. I told the sergeant to represent the company. He explained to me that this type of thing occurred not infrequently and that the Magistrate required a company officer or lawyer from the Post's Judge Advocate Department to come to court. It was obviously too late to find a legal representative, and I was the only company officer. I checked into class and received permission to leave. Fortunately, I was not in fatigues that day.

One of the things we were not taught at West Point was how to handle judicial matters. We were thoroughly immersed in learning how major battles were fought and won or lost, but we had no training in several areas of civilian life when it conflicted with the Army. We were instructed in mounted cavalry maneuvers, and this training continued through 1946. I guess nobody in the military wanted to get rid of all the horses we had. I was petrified to realize that I had to think for myself, which was a rare military situation. As I became older, I found out that you really had to adapt without reference to military doctrine.

When I reached the courtroom, I asked one of the policemen where my soldier was. He took me into an adjoining room where defendants were kept prior to their hearings. I found a reasonably well-dressed private about my age standing there with his occupation ribbons on. I questioned him about his background. He was born and raised in Brooklyn, New York, drafted into the Army, and sent overseas with the laundry company a few months after being sworn in. He had never been out of New York until he joined the Army and was returned to the United States. I was surprised that his basic training was so brief. It had taken place in 1945 when the fighting in Europe was finished. At any rate, when he went into town on a public bus, he sat on an empty front seat. The driver told him to move to the rear. He saw that the rear seats were filled, so he refused to do so. The driver stopped the bus at the first intersection where there was a policeman and had him arrested. I could see that being south of the Mason-Dixon Line made no difference to him. However, my very first lesson at West Point had to do with this situation, and I had many thoughts over the years as to how I would handle it if it ever came up. I had been prevented from registering at a hotel with several of my classmates in New York State because the desk agent asked if I was Jewish. They did not allow Jews into the hotel. Gregory Peck in *To Kill a Mockingbird* showed the same thing happening at that time. Sitting on bus front seats was the black equivalent.

The Judge sat on an elevated platform behind a lectern and wore judicial robes. He asked me for my name and relationship to the defendant. I responded that I was his company commander and had no idea as to why he was being tried. His response sounded like I expected. He said that I was obviously a Yankee or I would know what the segregation laws were in the South. I replied that I was born in Daytona Beach, Florida, which was a lot farther away from the Mason-Dixon Line than he was. I also included the fact that this company was dissolving and that the defendant should be discharged within the next few months. The Judge said that he would not put him in jail if I agreed to give him company punishment. I volunteered that he could be put on kitchen police if the Judge felt that was sufficient punishment. He suggested a month. I suggested a week, and we compromised at two weeks. KP was never to be used as punishment in my first days at Ft. Benning's Training class, but I thought that we needed KPs anyway, and I did not think that I could get a "not guilty" judgment out of this Judge. He directed the policeman to turn the soldier over to me and said that he would like to talk to me in Court Chambers after his last case, which was not more than fifteen minutes away.

When he went into his Chambers, he couldn't have been more cordial. He said that he would have sentenced the soldier to a month in jail except that he knew that I was not like the other officers who had come into his court, since I was a *real* Southerner. Would I like to have dinner with him and his two daughters at his house this coming Saturday? I asked him whether I could bring a friend since he said that he had two daughters. He agreed. I returned to the base having in my mind that I won my first case and hoped that there would not be another. When

I returned to the base, I found Bernie Janis, my classmate there, and invited him to go with me. He was delighted to accept.

The visit to Judge Shepherd's house was interesting. When we entered the house Saturday night, we were warmly greeted by the Judge's wife and the two daughters, Dottie and Christine (Crit). They were pretty and just slightly younger. He pointed out a large portrait painting in the living room of a woman which had a big cut through the painting's canvas. He said to Bernie that since he was from the North he should know that the cut was caused by one of his forebearers in the Union Army. He kept the picture there to remind him of the behavior of Yankee troops. I was speechless. However, after a shot of bourbon, the conversation became quite friendly and the dinner exceptional. Upon leaving, we invited the two girls to the Officers' Club the next Saturday night, and they gladly accepted. The Army was getting friendlier and friendlier. My luck had finally changed.

The following week of cooking school was in the large kitchen of Camp Lee, which fed over a thousand. One session of KP was assigned to each of us. When I was on my KP duty, I noticed a familiar face across from me. Since I was dressed in cook's whites, he didn't recognize me at first. He suddenly realized who I was and jumped up saying, "Lieutenant! What did you do?" I was happy to be recognized by my freed soldier.

Our dates on Saturday night were much more charming than we expected from our previous dinner at their home. Bernie said that he would not be able to meet with them the following week since he had to be in New York to attend a meeting at their club at which his father was being honored and made the club's new president. The girls said that they had never been to New York and would love to see it. Bernie suggested that I take the girls up there on the train, stay overnight at a hotel near his residence, and return to Virginia the next day. I agreed to take them if I could get a classmate to take over my company over the weekend and the upper echelon allowed it. I encountered no resistance to the deal but had to leave a day after Bernie since the meeting he was to be at was a day earlier than I could leave. We, of course, had to get the Judge's permission—which was granted. We reserved only one room at the hotel since I was to stay with Bernie.

Our trip to New York was pleasant, and we arrived in the city in the late afternoon. When we checked into the hotel on Fifty-Seventh Street, the lobby was full of ensigns—graduates from the Naval Academy. When they saw me come in with my two lady friends, they treated us like VIPs and invited us to have dinner with them in the hotel dining room. We did that without Bernie since he had been detained by friends of his family at his home. I took the girls' luggage to their room and was followed by several of the ensigns who came into the room with us. The girls insisted that I remain there with the ensigns. I had no objection to that and called Bernie to tell him I could not join him for a while. He said he had a few family members around and to come to his place at any time later that evening with the girls if possible. His residence was more than twenty blocks away. More than walking distance.

The hotel room was a large twin-bedded room with a couch and open floor space. It had a radio with a connection to music. Televisions were not yet popular. With the music on and a tray of hors-d'oeurves the ensigns provided, there was dancing along with another girl they had picked up in the lobby. We had a real party going. It was interesting enough to last several hours. The phone rang and I answered it. Hotel security said that the noise was bothering the other room occupants on the floor, and we had to quiet down. I tried to convey the message. It was certainly not well received, although one of the ensigns disappeared with the additional girl. The noise continued. A knock on the door was answered to a uniformed hotel guard who directed all of us to leave, except for the two lady residents. We agreed, but told him that we were out of uniform and needed a little time to exit. He disappeared. The music was turned back on. The remaining ensigns left, and I went into the bathroom to straighten up before leaving. Another knock of a probably annoyed security detail came. One of the girls said that we had all left and they had forgotten to turn off the music. The chain lock on the door was still on, but the guard was insistent on coming in to look. Crit ran into the bathroom and told me to stand in the bathtub. She jumped in and turned on the shower while taking off her sweater and reaching out of the curtain so that she could open the bathroom door. Dottie opened the chain lock and the guard came in, looked behind the sofa and under the beds, but found no one there. When he opened the bathroom door, the shower was running and a lady's bare arm was exposed, so he left the room quickly. When the room door was closed, I climbed out soaking wet. I said good night to the girls and left the room.

It was raining hard when I exited the hotel lobby. I took a taxi to Bernie's parents' apartment. That took some time since taxis in New York are scarce when it rains. However, it created an excuse for my appearance when Bernie's mother opened the door. She was obviously upset since my arrival time was about midnight. Her guests had left some time ago, and she had already gone to bed. Bernie was asleep. Mrs. Janis handed me a pair of pajamas and took my clothes, which were delivered to me dry and pressed in the early morning when I awoke.

The rest of the day was spent with the girls, showing them Manhattan. We had dinner that night in a restaurant, left the girls at the hotel, and went back to Petersburg in the morning.

When I returned to my company, I had orders to report to the Quartermaster Depot in Jeffersonville, Indiana, as soon as a replacement officer arrived to relieve me. That happened the next day and effectively broke up my relationship with the girls since I never again was assigned anywhere close to Petersburg. I did attend an officer's call before I left and volunteered to join the paratroops since it would pay me an extra $100 per month. Several of my classmates volunteered at the same session and probably for the same reason. I drove to Indiana in my own auto and arrived there the next day.

When I checked into the Depot, I was told that no living accommodations were available on the Post. The officer who checked me in said that I had a classmate stationed there and suggested that I contact him about outside quarters. When I found him, he suggested that I stay with him a few days until I found suitable quarters. Since he had been married a few weeks before, living with him was not feasible in a two-room apartment. I found one in New Albany, the adjoining community, and moved in.

The Depot handled Graves Registration equipment. It is a Quartermaster function to buy what caskets are necessary for burial of deceased Army personnel. The Depot handled other equipment as well, and I was given the loan of a motorcycle to get around. I liked the motorcycle until the evening I drove it within the Depot grounds. The front wheel went into a water-filled hole in the parking lot, creating a sudden stop and a trip over the handlebars to the ground. That cured me of my liking for motorcycles.

Life at the Depot was boring. There were no troops to train and insufficient duties to keep me busy. I suspected that the Depot would soon close, but it did not for several years. I had a tour of Louisville, which was across the river, and I took a weekend trip to Chicago where Zelda Klein, who had visited me at Hundredth Night at West Point, was matriculating at the

University of Chicago. She was happy at the school and seemed pleased with my visit. It was the second date we ever had even though we knew each other all our lives. Although I did not realize it at the time, it started a friendship which turned into an engagement a year or two later. My acceptance of parachute training arrived after my return to my Post. I was delighted to leave Graves Registration and drove directly to parachute school.

I arrived at Fort Benning in a brand-new Studebaker. It was a remarkably well-designed machine. From a distance, you could not tell which end was the front. The designer was reputed to be Herb Baker of Chicago, who was dating Zelda Klein at the time. Two weeks after I arrived in Georgia, I was returning to Fort Benning in Columbus, driving unusually carefully since I noticed that a local police car was on my tail. As I passed a road intersection, I was hit on the driver's side by a nondescript auto with such force that it threw me through the passenger side door. I was in good physical condition in those days, in process to becoming a paratrooper. Although I was stunned by the shock, I had no permanent injuries except some cuts and scratches on my face and hands and black-and-blue marks on my body. The following police car was able to stop before hitting my car in front of them. They saw me getting to my feet and went after the driver of the other car who was either very drunk or shaken up by the accident. He had apparently come downhill through a stop sign at the corner. The officers picked him out of his car and used their billy clubs to beat him unconscious. I was shocked at the brutality and asked them to quit. The man was black and, according to the police, had been picked up for drunken driving enough times that they recognized him. They drove me back to the base as soon as another police car arrived. I was told to be in magistrate's court the next morning.

I borrowed a car from one of my classmates and went to the court. The difference between the Virginia court and this one was substantial. The prisoner was brought in shackled. The Judge was familiar enough with him to address him by name without looking at the transcript in front of him. I was asked whether this was the man who ran into me. I felt sorry for him and testified that I had not had a good look at him since the officers who had witnessed the accident were beating him so that I could not see his face. The Judge said that this man had been convicted by him several times and that I was lucky to be alive, let alone not badly injured. He apparently was not impressed with me. I did not receive an invitation to his house as I had from Judge Shepherd.

Since my car was destroyed beyond hope of repair, I was contacted by my insurance agent who offered me a new one. He could not get another Studebaker since there was a long waiting list for them. He had a four-door Dodge available with an automatic fluid transmission—a great advance in automotive engineering at that time. I accepted and used the Dodge for more than four years in the Unites States and Germany. When I was transferred out of Germany, I sold it for more than the value of it when I received it. It stayed in excellent running condition with little maintenance for close to one hundred thousand miles.

Back at Fort Benning, I was engaged in learning how to jump out of planes and survive. It was quite interesting since we went through training with former Nazi paratroops that had been given passes to Argentina. They captured the island of Crete from the air. Peron wanted them probably to take the Falklands. Our Army wanted to change the training manuals to provide for military cover by quartermaster ground troops instead of infantry when drops were made. That meant to me that we would have to make cooks, supply troops, and other service personnel into combat ready forces. I did not like the idea but when you are a lieutenant you are not asked questions as to whether you like the curriculum or not.

We were told that we would join the Eighty-Second Airborne Division, then being transferred from Lawton Field to Fort Bragg, when we had completed our required six jumps. We were assigned to Monmouth, New Jersey, instead of Fort Bragg. Since Monmouth wasn't far from Wilkes-Barre, I made a date with Zelda and was able to visit Wilkes-Barre until shipped overseas.

My stay at Monmouth lasted about one month. We had plenty of free time since there were no assigned duties. When we four paratroopers left the Brooklyn Navy Yard for Bremerhaven, we were assigned to the hold of a converted cargo ship converted into a troop transport. The boat was the *General Buckner*. We were assigned cots in the hold and were subjected to a lengthy voyage in the company of a full hold of replacement troops. Our government's policy was to rid Europe of all active combat forces since they would be harder to control as occupation troops. They may have had a good point.

One of the good things about travel on this military vessel was the PX. Cigarettes were fifty cents per carton, and there was no rationing. Card games were everywhere, and I noticed that a continuing craps game was going on at most hours. The food was passable, and we could comment on it because we were not only paratroopers but also graduates of Camp Lee's Cooks and Baker's School. The weather was rough, but I do not recall anyone getting seasick. Cooped up as we were, that would have made the trip almost unbearable. After many days of this, we landed in Germany. The troops were transported by buses from Bremerhaven to Marburg. This was the town selected to be the replacement depot. My car was delivered to me from the boat, and we went directly there. We spent a good deal of time on the troop transport discussing our training at Fort Benning. The arrival at Fort Benning was much different than our initial one after graduation leave. We were only six Quartermasters checking in. Our assigned quarters were better than previously. Our first training day was in an auditorium filled with both officers and enlisted men. The world situation was presented first from the stage. I did not understand why, and I still have no idea why. We were also given an oral summary of what our training would be with the caveat that we could drop out of the course at any time if we wished. The class makeup was explained. We had former German (Nazi) troops who were brought up from Argentina. They had captured the Island of Crete with no outside support. They had moved to Argentina with Vatican passes and Peron's request. I supposed that Peron was getting ready to occupy the Falkland Islands, which Argentina had been claiming that they were its property for many years. One speaker stated that the Middle East was a hotbed and the British were planning to leave Israel, which would ignite a war. I thought that we were being indoctrinated into the belief that although our major wars in Europe and Asia were finished, there were always more little ones ahead in which paratroops could be necessary. Service troops would be necessary, and the Infantry Troops would no longer be dropped with aerial supply drops. This would require Quartermaster troops for security with the drops. The game was changing. New manuals would be issued.

We had been split up into "sticks"—which groups were assigned to the DC-3s, the aerial delivery planes at that time. The officers were told to buy suitable boots, both to train in and to use in the six jumps we would be required to make. We were to initially receive physical training, including a parachute drop from a high tower that reminded me of one I had been in at a County Fair. I purchased a beautiful pair of Cordovan leather boots, which looked great to me in the store mirror. Everyone else of the officers bought the standard ones, which were much cheaper. Danny Graham, Jack Schuman, Ted Upland, and I were each assigned to a separate group. We had the joint exercises together, which included jumping off a twelve-foot platform into a square box of wood shavings. Most of us jumped off the back of a slow-moving truck platform onto a dirt road. An instructor showed us how safe the chutes were on a contraption consisting of ropes hanging down from beams which were at a height of about twenty feet. We were shocked to see him hook the ropes in various directions to show that they would straighten themselves out if mixed up in the initial windblast. He asked for a volunteer to do it and received no response. So he went back a second time and secured the ropes in an even more odd way, jumped again, and you could hear his neck snap. He had injured himself badly and had to be carried off in the back of a truck to our hospital. We heard later that he was dead. It had a very sobering effect on all of us.

After several days of exercises, we were assigned to our first jump, which was to take place at Lawton Field across the river separating the base from the practice jump area. Going into the mess hall that morning, one of our guys brought a bottle of bourbon with him. We had steak and eggs and a shot of bourbon. It was a crazy thing to do, but no one stopped us. We had packed our own chutes the day before and put them on.

When we entered the plane, the copilot asked me if I wanted to go first or last. He said that officers always went either way. I was not sure that I had enough nerve to be last, so I went first. The young private behind me was instructed to examine the cord which was fastened to the back of my chute and a cord in the plane. I saw no purpose in this since I felt that the string would certainly break from the pressure. However, I discovered the hard way that the airflow on leaving the plane was such that, unless the release strap was immediately severed from the plane, the time of the release was affected so that you might hit the tail or strut of the wing. Today's planes have drop platforms, which are safer— but in 1947 we had none of those planes available. I talked to the private behind me and asked him for the sake of conversation whether he had learned anything from our inspirational lecture. He said he had. He wanted to jump in all the places mentioned except in Israel since there were too many Jews there, and he didn't want any part of them. He knew that none of them were paratroopers since they were too yellow to jump. I responded by telling him that I was one of those guys he hated, and I seriously hoped that his chute wouldn't open on his first jump today. I'm not religious, but my wish partially came true since he twisted his ankle when he landed and had to be carried to the waiting truck for the injured. I never saw him again on our next five flights or glider that we had to land in. I was unable to determine whether he was seriously injured or not and really did not care.

My beautiful boots were obviously not made for jumping out of DC-3s. The air had twisted the opening cord close enough to one of my legs that it caught onto one of the lacing hooks and tore the leather to a point where it was not economical to have repairs made. My next jumps were in regular boots, and I had no trouble with the cords. I did have a black-and-blue mark on my chest from the opening shock. When I showed it to an instructor, he told me to tape a sponge over the mark and it would disappear. It was excellent advice since it cushioned the shock to the point where there was only pressure felt and no pain. I even reached the point after two jumps where I enjoyed it. I felt that when I received my elevated monthly paycheck, I had made the correct decision to become a paratrooper.

We had been informed that we were to be assigned to the

Eighty-Second Airborne Division, which was then moving to Fort Bragg from our post. We were held in Columbus, Georgia, for about a month. I used the time to visit my Atlanta cousin, Bud Weiss, and was a guest at the Standard Club. The parachute wings on my uniform were the subject of conversation with some of the members I met. Senator Herman Talmadge and his aide, a Mr. Levy, stopped at our table and asked me how I liked Fort Benning. I told him that I liked it well, but not living in Georgia since it was considered an anti-Semitic state. And anyway, why was he at the Standard Club, probably the oldest Jewish social club in the nation. He surprised me by saying that he had been invited to join the Standard Club and ate there regularly with his aide, Mr. Levy, who was smiling at the conversation. He said that he took care of the Senator's finances and had been with the Senator for many years. He never heard him make an anti-Semitic remark except to the media when he was coming up for elections. He received extra votes from the farm country that way. I was getting further education.

After several weeks in Georgia with no assignments, we had been told that our destination would not be the Eighty-Second, but Germany. We would be held at Fort Monmouth, New Jersey. Since this location is close to New York City, we decided to go in to see the sights. We were delighted to learn that Army was to play a football game with Columbia in New York, and a call to the Academy ticket office informed us as to where we could pick up admission tickets to the stadium. We did not expect the game to amount to much since Army still had the strongest team in the nation, and Columbia wasn't even rated.

The game was all Columbia's from the first play. The cadets in the stands were unbelievably silent. We were all reading sports pages in those days, and Columbia's coach, Lou Little, was praised as having made his team quite efficient. Against Army? No way.

We had never seen an Army team lose from after our entrance year until now. The Army team was treated at West Point like junior Gods with their own portion of the Mess Hall, excused from parades, specially tutored in subjects where they were weak, and rarely received any demerits. We thought that Lou Little had created a major sports miracle. Unfortunately, things were changing. The war was over and the pressures, under which we studied, had been lifted to a point which included the football team.

During the month we were held at Monmouth, I was allowed to go to my family's home in Pennsylvania. I did so several times. During one of these visits, I dated Zelda since she had finished her Chicago education, and was on the junior social circuit. She was rumored to have become engaged to a Scranton physician, and she was involved in the amateur theater circuit, which included Wilkes College's Drama School. She had the lead in *Antigone* and received a best actress award from the College. It has always been in my office where it stands today and will stand as long as I last. This slack period turned out to be important in my life since my feelings about Zelda had changed substantially. I never thought of marriage in those days. I was twenty-one years old, and marriage was far from my mind. I had an Army career to look forward to. My great-grandmother's opinion of me as a "General Nuisance" had to be overcome.

We were finally shipped to Germany on the *General Buckner*, a well-used Army transport ship, which was fully loaded with troops. As second lieutenants, we traveled in the hold on bunks with the enlisted men. I have no idea why it took so long to reach Bremerhaven. Probably ten days, but it felt like a month. I was fortunate to have my Dodge shipped on the same boat. Since the weather was inclement I rarely came out on the deck. The days were spent at poker games and craps. The PX sold cigarettes for five cents per pack. The food available was very good but we had no appetites for it. By the time we docked in Bremerhaven we were starved for outdoor activities. We had Marburg as our destination and drove right to the replacement depot.

My first surprise in Germany was at the highway we were on. It was the Autobahn. We had no roads in the United States to compare with it. It was a highway like I saw in the 1939 World's Fair's Trylon and Perisphere display of Worlds to Come. There was an Army fuel depot clearly marked on the way, and I filled my tank at twelve cents per gallon. I paid with American currency but was told by the attendant that he could only take it since we were just off the boat. He suggested that we stop at the American Express office in town to change our currency to Occupation currency. There were plenty of directional signs to our offices in Marburg. It was pleasant to have everything in excellent order. There were no signs of war damage anywhere on our route.

In Marburg we attended a meeting with other newly arrived officers and were made to feel at home. We were told that our assignments would be given to us in a few days. In the meantime we were free to explore Marburg and other sites but were warned not to go into the outskirts without arms because there had been recent incidents of a not too serious nature by juveniles who were not happy that we were occupying their country. Since it was the day before Thanksgiving the weather was cold and wet. We wore our raincoats and sweaters and were issued pistols with ammunition which fit nicely in the pockets. We were assigned quarters in former German officer's quarters close to the middle of town.

Danny Graham and I decided to stretch our legs after the evening meal. Jack Schuman and Ted Upland did not want to go out in the darkened streets. The street lights were not working but we had flashlights. With our loaded pistols in our pockets we felt invincible especially with paratroop boots. We were looking for trouble although we didn't admit it even to ourselves. We walked together for a while but Danny was interested in the stone work on some of the undamaged buildings. He was also trying to find the church where Martin Luther posted his objections to Roman Catholicism to which Danny had converted at West Point. He wanted me to do it, but I told him that I had enough religious training already.

While walking separated from Danny, I noticed the figure of a man coming toward me about a block away. He stopped at his corner and seemed to talk to another man. In the darkness of the night, I couldn't see more than the two figures that disappeared. I called back to Danny who was behind me, and he started to run to join me. I turned around to see where he was and was surprised when I felt two hands—one around my neck and one over my right hand, which was holding my pistol. He had a strong grip and pulled the pistol away from my hand. His companion came up behind Danny and seized his pistol as well. In Russian, they told us to come with them and led us with pistols pointed at us to a large house not more than a hundred yards away.

Danny and I had been in the Russian class at the Academy and could understand a little of what they were saying. We never thought we would use it, but here it was in Germany on our first night there. Colonel Beukema, in-charge of the language course and a classmate of Eisenhower, had told us that we needed to be prepared to speak Russian since he was convinced that they would move their army to the English Channel. We couldn't believe that we might be in the vanguard of that movement. What else could we believe? I never thought I would use the language, but I was wrong again. It sure came in handy that night.

We were ordered upstairs to a large room in which were thirty soldiers in civilian and military clothes. They were Jewish Russian Army deserters making their way west to go to Israel, probably through the Bremerhaven Port. They were overjoyed to have me, a Jewish American, celebrate the evening with them. The United Nations had voted to allow the Jews to set up a separate country in Palestine that day. This group had set up a buffet with Vodka, naturally. We were treated as honored visitors at their celebration. Danny was so delighted that he started to do a Russian Kazotsky and yelled that his conversion was possibly to the wrong faith. We had a few drinks and spent over an hour getting information that we knew would be appreciated by our intelligence if we ever got out of there alive. After wining and dining us, they gave us our pistols still loaded, and several of them accompanied us to within a few blocks of our quarters.

When we reported the incident to the officer in charge the next morning, he probably smelled the alcohol on our breaths. Neither of us thought that he believed us. In his position, I don't think I would have, either. I hope the Russian deserters got to where they were going. I believe that the incident gave Danny his idea of going into military intelligence, which he did, eventually ending up with three stars.

The next day was spent reading the newspapers in the morning. We had been away from all news both printed and over the radio for two weeks. I was impressed the way that the war crimes trials in Nuremberg were proceeding and was surprised that the Nazi Camp Commander of Dachau was named Weiss and had been convicted. We had a long Thanksgiving weekend in front of us with no plans. I suggested that we drive to Dachau to see the camp. With gas at twelve cents per gallon and liquor available at the local Class 6 store at bargain prices, it would not cost us much. Jack Schuman and Danny agreed to go with me. We were told that the camp was yellow lined during the trial so that we couldn't get in. We needed the liquor to bribe the entrance guard. When we arrived at the gate, the liquor not only got us in but the guard was our guide as well. There were no American troops in Dachau since it was Thanksgiving Day.

Our guide was Polish but understood some Russian. Probably more than we did. He was a prisoner at the time of liberation. He had been in a prison maintenance group and was very familiar with the grounds and the tortures inflicted on the inmates. Hitler wanted a photographic record kept of all activities that occurred at the camp. The photos were at the trial, but copies were left in a little wooden shack near the camp's entrance. He showed us pictures of piles of naked bodies, too many to burn, that the Nazis had in the camp when the American troops came in. He also had pictures of the tortures being performed on the inmates. Several were so disgusting that I have difficulty even now describing them. The hanging bar was shown outside men's barracks where naked women who were about to give birth were hung from their wrists with their legs tied together so that they would die in agony, screaming while their relatives in the near prison buildings had the windows opened so they could hear the screams. There were pictures of naked men hanging with their penises exposed, and the police dogs biting them off with the guards smiling. There were hundreds more. We were taken to the sites where these tortures occurred. When I looked up, I could see the windows of the apartment buildings overlooking the camp. That meant that the neighbors were witnesses to these amazingly sadistic acts. The guard told us that the prosecutors in the trials were having trouble getting witnesses since there were almost none. He said that when American troops burst into the camp, they killed every guard in site. The American troop commander rounded up all of the occupants of the neighboring buildings and used them to clean up the camp. They objected strenuously, saying that they had no knowledge of what went on there. In the forty months I was in Germany, I heard that same lame excuse dozens of times. I left Germany believing that the Nazis had the blessing and complicity of the general population. We drove back to Marburg that evening in agreement, but sick to our stomachs.

We spent the rest of the weekend in Marburg, mainly sightseeing, and we found the church that started the wave of resistance to the Roman Catholics. Out of that manifesto grew numerous sects and branches of Christianity, many of which settled in the United States, particularly in Southern Pennsylvania. On Monday, we followed our orders and went to Darmstadt for a new beginning in military service for the type of which we were ill-prepared.

Having had both good and bad receptions to our occupation zone, we awaited our assignments. Someone in the Pentagon decided that we could be used as MPs to rehabilitate about six hundred convicted and incarcerated prisoners. We had had no MP training. However, we were all in excellent physical condition and looked forward to trying to do something constructive for our Country. We were assigned to the military post in Darmstadt to receive our troops. We were shocked with the appointment when we arrived. It became quite difficult as time passed. I was lucky enough to volunteer as Supply Officer in charge of supplying a group of convicted criminals who had learned more than I ever knew about crimes. An inventory of our supplies revealed that we were short more than $200 worth of sheets. I had never personally received the sheets and was not supply officer when they were supposed to have arrived.

After our first murder in the barracks our first night on the post, we never went unarmed. The .45 caliber pistols issued are heavy and hard to use. But we needed them not for the German population but for battle-hardened troops too dangerous to send back to Leavenworth. A first lieutenant, Irv Davis, was sent in to be temporary company commander. He was supposed to have troop experience. Nothing changed. Captain Moore was sent in to run things. His specialty was as a supervisor in charge of large dining halls. We set up patrols over twenty-four-hour periods, and things did quiet down somewhat. I was assigned the job of VD Control Officer. As a virgin (at twenty-two in those days, it was not so unusual), all my lectures came out of Army manuals. Our VD rate was in excess of 100 percent per annum. The five of us decided that we needed somebody to help us out in our predicament. Danny Graham suggested that we each request to be transferred but the requests be submitted collectively. I did not like the idea, but I went along with the group. The requests were given to Irv Davis who may have delivered them. I received a telephone call from the Colonel in charge of our sector who wanted to destroy mine, which was the only one submitted. I, of course, agreed to withdraw the request and was shocked that Danny had set me up.

Sometimes things work out in your favor, and sometimes not. I was summoned to Bad Tolz, First Division Headquarters, before a board for a hearing on the matter. Before the hearing, I received a visit from Danny Graham, the brains behind the withdrawal request who pointed out that if I told the entire truth that we all agreed to submit letters, we could be guilty of conspiracy and subject to severe punishment. If I stood alone, the worst that would happen is that I would be reassigned. He stated that he knew one of the officers on the Disciplinary Board and assured me that the only question I would be asked was whether I had made the transfer request. He was correct. He never acknowledged that he had not submitted all the requests, but just mine. The result was that I received a zero efficiency report from Captain Moore, and Danny had a glowing one. He applied for Military Intelligence and ended his career with three stars as Chief of Military Intelligence. My career was badly damaged by this.

Darmstadt had been so badly punished by bombing that you could stand on top of a three-foot-high stone wall and overlook most of the city. Some of the municipal buildings were standing, and I suppose that the reason that the walled area in which we were to conduct our mission was kept intact was to be utilized by our troops. We had no idea that we were to be a halfway house for American convicted criminals that the Army wanted to rehabilitate. How the Quartermaster General ever agreed to that has always been puzzling to me. We were paratroopers, not MPs or trained prison guards.

The four of us worked out the various functions of each platoon forming the company. We all had very little experience with companies in the United States, and there were no written directives given to us. The general idea was that we could take 600 prisoners and turn them into an operating supply company of about 150 men. That would help out the prison system. To my knowledge, it had not been tried before. We weren't too unhappy with the assignment because we figured that, even if we made mistakes, no one could tell.

After the first load of prisoners arrived, we changed our minds about the unit's possibility of success. After all, it was only a supply company, but we all split the training duties. We decided that the way to keep order was to keep the troops so busy that they could not get into trouble. That meant reveille at the crack of daylight with several mile runs, and frequent inspections of the troops' quarters to see if any unauthorized activities were going on. These guys had been let out of a prison environment, and they were almost uncontrollable. Our pistols were always with us, even in bed under the pillow.

My first night of guard duty was one I'll always remember. I heard a dog barking constantly, and having grown up with dogs, I knew that it was in trouble. It wasn't until daybreak that I discovered that the dog had been pulled up on a harness to the top of the flagpole in the central area. It occurred to me that it had to have been put there to distract me from something going on in the barracks. An investigation confirmed my worst fears. There had been a murder of one of the prisoners by one of the others. Naturally, no one admitted to seeing it. The only good thing that came out of the evening was the dog, a female miniature Spitz, which adopted me and remained with me for fifteen more years until her death. I named her Josie. She was smart enough to become a watchdog so that I could sleep much more comfortably. She slept under my bed and accompanied me on guard details.

The supply sergeant I had put in charge had a history of being a supply sergeant in an infantry company. I made frequent inspections of supplies. I reported the shortage of the two hundred sheets previously mentioned to our first lieutenant, Irv Davis. As a result, I was fined $200 since that was the value of the sheets. It was deducted from my pay automatically. I objected to this since our pay wasn't that great and there was probably an error in the bookkeeping entries when the supplies were received. The sheets were supposed to be there when we arrived. I never found out what happened to the sheets or if there had been a theft. It would have been extremely difficult to get them out of the Post unless they went out in the trash, and there was no evidence of that. It could have happened at night when I was distracted by the barking dog.

I think that anyone entering a new job feels the same worry that I had. We agreed that someone in the Pentagon figured out that there were too many troops in our penal area, and who would be better to try to rehabilitate them than Quartermaster paratroopers that they couldn't figure out what to do with. Our analysis was probably wrong, but we guessed that it might be an excellent opportunity to get promoted faster. No one wants to do that more than second lieutenants, the Army's lowest rank. We felt like we were going into a Roman amphitheater to be eaten by the lions, but we had no idea how we were going to be able to beat the odds. After all, these troops, all convicted criminals, were combat experienced and we were not.

When we entered the military post in Darmstadt, we had driven through one of the most bombed-out towns in Germany. It probably was selected for reciprocal raids for the German bombing of Coventry. Although the city was destroyed, the military post was not touched. Our quarters were better furnished and more comfortable than the ones we had occupied in the United States. Our first week was spent organizing the 150 prisoners, which were our initial group, into sections to be supervised. At least one of us was always on duty day or night. During daylight hours, all of us were on duty.

Frankfurt on Main was our closest large city and military post. It showed a little damaged landscape and was close to a large officer's club in Frankfurt's IG Farben headquarters building. All four powers were represented there. Numerous swaps of merchandise took place in the club on an individual basis. With the amount of alcohol being consumed the atmosphere was quite friendly. I felt that the Russians were sizing us up as we were sizing up them. Contacts were made that would later come in handy when we wanted certain German Army Russian prisoners, and they wanted gold and watches.

As our new troops arrived, they received complete medical examinations showing that we had an extremely high venereal disease rate. We drew straws to see who would become the VD Control officer. I lost. This meant that I would have to deliver lectures on a subject of which I had little knowledge. Our company had the largest VD rate in the zone. It was more than 100 percent. That meant that many who had been cured of the disease contracted it again. It also meant that when a soldier was allowed to leave the base for any reason, he had to take the contraceptive I would personally hand him. Truckloads of German girls came to the gate almost every day. They were hungry. My lesson here was that we had better never lose a war. I believe that *no* German women had escaped being raped by Russian or U.S. troops. We were told that the Pope had requested the removal of our black troop companies for this reason.

It had been my practice to telephone my parents every Sunday afternoon. The telephone service to the United States was good. I had met an American lady who worked as a nurse in the Red Cross station near Darmstadt. She visited me on weekends when she could and I was not on duty at the time. Her name was Ginnie, and she came from Virginia. There were few American girls around so she was quite a prize in the Darmstadt area. I thought that she would like to meet my folks on the phone one Sunday and did so. My mother ended our conversation with the advice that I marry Zelda Klein in the near future. That ended the relationship with Ginnie. I was a new lieutenant and couldn't have been happier single. I wasn't very sad at the chain of events.

Subsequent conversations with Zelda led to an agreement to marry. American civilians were not allowed into the zone unless belonging to an agency approved by the government or was the spouse of a military person stationed there. I thought that I would not be eligible to marry her for some time until the ban was lifted. My mother had a friend—Dan Flood, our local Pennsylvania Congressman—who was on the Military Affairs

Committee in Congress. He was not in Congress when I was appointed, but was at this time. He obtained special permission allowed to my mother and Zelda's mother to come into the zone for marriage purposes. The fathers were not allowed. A wedding date was set, and they arrived in the zone about a month later.

Lt. and Mrs. Norman E. Weiss are shown at the reception which followed their wedding at Darmstadt, Germany. The sword used for cutting their wedding cake formerly belonged to a high Nazi official.

LT. NORMAN E. WEISS TAKES MISS ZELDA KLEIN AS BRIDE

Miss Zelda Klein, daughter of Mr. and Mrs. Ben Klein of 377 West Academy Street, and Lt. Norman E. Weiss, son of Mr. and Mrs. Aaron Weiss of 36 East Dorrance Street, Kingston, were married at Darmstadt, Germany, where Lt. Weiss is serving with the Army of Occupation.

According to German law, a civil wedding ceremony was performed on Saturday afternoon, March 6, at the "burgomeister's." The religious ceremony took place on Sunday afternoon, March 7, in Frankfurt, Germany. Chaplain Blumenthal, formerly of Huntington, W. Va., officiated. A number of friends of Lt. Weiss attended the ceremony, among them Major Alebrode, the judge advocate of the Darmstadt Post.

Following the ceremony, a reception was held at the Officers' Country Club at Langen. An attractive 50-pound wedding cake beautifully decorated for the occasion was sent by Mr. and Mrs. Reuben H. Levy of 33 Reynolds Street, Kingston. The cake was sent air express from the Wilkes-Barre-Scranton Airport at Avoca and arrived in Germany two days later. Shipping charges for the cake, which served about 200 guests, amounted to $72.45.

The bride is a graduate of Wyoming Seminary and University of Chicago. Lt. Weiss was graduated from Wyoming Seminary and West Point Military Academy.

Mrs. Weiss and Mrs. Klein, who left about a month ago for Germany to attend the wedding, will sail today on the New Amsterdam from Rotterdam for home.

During the month before the wedding, we had received our new commanding officer, Captain Moore. When he arrived at the post, none of us saw him except Irv Davis. He left word that he had a bad cold and could not meet with any of us. We wondered what life would be like with our new Captain. The fact was after Irv Davis had met him and was uncomplimentary did not surprise us because, now, Irv would not be in charge. I hoped that I could transfer out of our company not because of the new boss, but because of the nature of the troops that we had to train and the perceived danger of having my new wife to be quartered outside but near base. I had discussed this with Danny who was full of ideas. He suggested that we each put in a request for transfer at the same time, which would put pressure on our captain to transfer at least one of us out, and it could be me. I agreed to do this if every one of us went along. Danny said he would take care of this and promised to submit all the requests at one time. I prepared mine and gave it to him. As it turned out, Danny submitted only my request.

During the next month, I was kept quite busy in the routine matters to which I had been assigned. I received a telephone call from the Colonel in Frankfurt in charge of our Post. I had met him at one of the joint Officers' Club gatherings and found him to be the kind of officer I'd like to be. He had been called by our Captain and wanted to question me about the letter of transfer request. I was surprised that he had not received any of the others. He said that he had no knowledge that there were others. He suggested that I withdraw the request since it would affect my efficiency rating by our captain. I had never heard about efficiency ratings, but agreed to do so. When I saw Danny, I questioned him about the other submissions—which he said had been delivered to his knowledge since he gave them to Irv Davis. He assumed that Davis had done that. The Colonel called me again about a week later and said that, because of the nature of our training, I would be questioned about the request which was now at Battalion Headquarters. I questioned Danny about this, and he stated that there was no problem since he had taken care of the matter at Battalion headquarters and all they would ask me was if I had submitted the application. He warned me to not mention the other applications, saying that it would look like a conspiracy if I did, which would be a lot worse than a transfer request. He said that he knew one of the officers on the board and was confident that they would ask me only one question which was whether I had submitted the form. He was correct. The transfer request was granted.

Before I left Darmstadt, my wedding took place in the Darmstadt Rathaus and in Frankfurt, at the Sondheim Chapel of the remaining Synagogue. The chaplain who performed the service was sent from Berlin on orders of General Maxwell Taylor, currently the West Point Superintendent, the senior American officer and who was in Germany at the time. Ours was the first American wedding in occupied Germany. Jack Schuman, my best man, told me that Taylor sent flowers along with the chaplain and a congratulatory note. While he was my West Point Superintendent, he had predicted that I would marry the girl I had invited to visit during Hundredth Night celebration. He was right. Zelda, with our mothers, accompanied us to the Mayor's office. He performed the ceremony in accordance with German law. Walking down the hall to his office, we passed a line of pictures of past mayors at one of which Anna Klein stopped and asked my mother to read the name. My mother's job as a Phys Ed instructor in the Wilkes-Barre school system required her to teach one class, which she did. It was German. In the Mayor's office, she questioned the mayor as to who was in the portrait. He replied, and Anna Klein said that he looked like a cousin of her mother who had left Germany in 1932 and settled in Chicago. He had been in the fur business. The mayor said that he had to take down a picture of Albert Einstein who had been raised in a village contiguous to Darmstadt. Since he was Jewish, he was regarded as an enemy of the Reich. It was a brief but successful wedding. Zelda went there in her athletic socks. She left after the ceremony with her two escorts to the guesthouse in which they were staying. I went back to work. German law required a civil wedding to be legal. A religious one is possible but not necessary. Both ladies were insistent that we not stay together until a religious ceremony was performed. The closest place was in Frankfurt and the ceremony was set at the next day.

The evening wedding reception was held the day of the civil ceremony in a former German officers' club. I invited all the officers at the base. Commissary food purchased for the occasion and a full orchestra cost me twenty-one cartons of cigarettes, which Zelda had brought in her trunk, and $150. The wedding cake was sent to us by air and delivered to the club. It was shipped with a cellophane window. There were more than a hundred well-wishing notes scribbled on the box. We left the party, and I slept in my room at the bachelor's quarters that night. When I walked into the officers' mess the next morning alone, the regular noise over which you could hardly carry a conversation normally was deadly quiet. I invited everyone who could to meet in Frankfurt for the religious ceremony. Most did.

The ceremony was held in the Sondheim Chapel of the Frankfurt Synagogue the next morning. I had told Jack Schuman of the interview I had with General Taylor before Hundredth Night to postpone my punishment tour to meet Zelda at West Point. His comment was that if he allowed it, I would probably marry the girl. Jack brought in a bouquet of flowers with a card attached which said: "Congratulations. I told you so.

Maxwell Taylor." Jack may have made up the card since Taylor was transferring to Berlin to take over the Army from General Lucius Clay about that time. It struck us as funny, as were the sabers held over us as we left the chapel. Jack said, "You never had a saber in a ceremony at West Point." He was right. We drove to Berchtesgarden after the ceremony where Paul Trostle, in charge of running special services, had contracted to have the Berchtesgaden Hof, which Hitler had built to house VIPs like Mussolini, cleaned up for officers' vacation use. We were the hotel's only guests for a week. However, the dining room and orchestra were in operation for most of the week, and we had wonderful skiing conditions every day on the local slopes.

When we returned to Darmstadt from Berchtesgaden I received orders to report to Major Amdur of the Military Police at Giessen. I had no regrets at leaving Darmstadt. My transfer to Giessen was a relief to me. I guessed that some of the officers in Darmstadt had guilty consciences over my reprimand and transfer. After a delightful wedding dinner held at the former Wehrmacht officers club, Paul Trostle said that the week at the Berctesgardener Hof (Hitler's favorite hotel equipped for Nazi special visitors) was undergoing renovation, but he arranged that we would be the only residents of the hotel during my week of leave.

At Giessen, I was assigned to a refrigeration truck company, which was busy carrying supplies from Bremerhaven to Berlin and other parts of the American Zone. The commanding officer was Larry Mansfield from Mansfield, Ohio. He left the company to return to Ohio, leaving me in charge. Junior officers were in very short supply after the war so that it was not unusual to assign a lieutenant to run a company. The base commander was Col. McAfee who stated that I was to have several extra duties such as Officers Club operation, plaintiff officer during minor trials, and battalion training officer, known as an S-3. There was very little time left to spend with my new wife, and that worked out since she applied for, and received, a position as a clerk breaking down supplies to be distributed by my company's refrigeration vans. The information allowed me to schedule movements in a timely manner.

The battalion training job wasn't too difficult. All combat troops had been sent back to the States, so what we had were unseasoned for the most part. To build up morale, my wife, who had had considerable drama and theater training, decided to put on a stage performance of a then currently running play, the title of which was *Post Road*. On the night of the performance, I called for a battalion formation and marched the troops downtown to the theater where the play was to be performed. We had a full house. Before the curtain went up, I went backstage to congratulate my wife. She informed me that a bit part player had fallen and injured his ankle so that he could not perform his part as a New York State Trooper. I filled in to be his substitute on the spot and changed clothes backstage. When I appeared in front of our troops, you could hear the jeers and cheers a long way away. I thought that the visiting general felt that this was a marvelous way to increase morale. He arranged to have a cocktail party for the post officers, and I was invited to help serve the drinks.

The success of the battalion training and a lucky few convictions obtained at the court martials caused considerable praise from Colonel McAfee. I requested to be relieved as Club Officer since I was not able to get more than a few hours' sleep every night. He stated that the club was running at a deficit. If I could turn it around and put it in a profit mode, he would consider my request. I remembered basic officer instruction, which stated that when you were required to perform an act, you looked to the top noncom available to do it for you. So I requested information from the club NCO as to how you could make a profit. He said that while he was stationed in England some time previously, his club ran at a profit. It was caused by slot machines (which were legal there), and he knew of no restrictions in Germany. He called his friend who, luckily for us, was still in his club job and had available used machines to sell. He sent us one on the next cargo plane to Germany, and we installed it immediately. The machine was so profitable that we had enough money to pay for it in a few weeks. I renewed my request to be let out of Officers Club duties, and the request was granted.

The Russians blockaded Berlin so that we were forced to rely on aerial shipments of supplies. Rumor had it that we were to break through with food shipments if the airborne shipments were insufficient. All Army females, including civilian wives, were requested to leave the base preparatory to returning to the States. I walked into the quarters to which we were assigned a short time after this notice to discover my wife wearing an ammunition bandolier, fully loaded, and carrying a carbine. She said she had no compunctions to shoot Russians if she had to, but was not leaving. I tried to dissuade her, but realized that she was probably readier for combat than I was.

She had several buddies among the Army wives, one of whom was Isabelle Webb. They had taken their carbine training together. I told her that seeing that she was serious about joining the infantry, what she and Isabelle Webb needed was pistols. The only pistols available from ordinance were .45s. I didn't think that they would even hold them, but I took them out to the pistol range to show them how the pistols worked and how to fire them. After the usual Army training of showing them how to load the gun, strip it for cleaning, and warning them never to point it at anyone unless they intended to shoot at them, I fired a number of rounds into the target. My wife was next. She complained of the strong kick but hit the target, although not accurately. I then handed the gun to Isabelle. She fired six shots, and I could not see whether she hit the target. When I went up to the target to inspect it, all her shots were in the black and centered. She was laughing at me, and with good reason. She was an army brat. Her father was on the Army pistol team and taught her how to shoot a variety of weapons, including a .45.

President Truman decided that we would not go against the Russians since the airlift was working to our surprise. With little left to do on the base, Col. McAfee assigned me to put together a platoon out of the training battalion, move the platoon around the Mannheim Depot which contained many unissued German weapons to see how they were getting out. There was a suspicion that they were. There was a suspicion that they were going to Israel to replace the British weapons which had been turned over to the Arabs. I remembered that I couldn't find the missing sheets at Darmstadt. I thought I might redeem myself in this way. I jumped at the chance. I was assigned to check security at Mannheim.

The assignment to Mannheim required that I station members of the platoon to remain concealed in the forest surrounding the depot. They were to intercept all persons entering or leaving the openings and bring them to me for questioning. Our first day's catch amounted to six people, all of whom were coming or going from the depot on legitimate business. Our subsequent days during the first week brought similar replies. I was suspicious of the train traffic, which consisted of coal cars passing through the depot loaded with coal to be used in Czechoslovakia. Other cars loaded with special clay called Kaolin were also going through in the other direction. This substance was utilized in the manufacture of china. The cars were sealed shut, and there was no sign of seal breakage or removal from them or the cartons in the warehouses.

We had camped on the ground in a forested area. Our food was C rations, for which we had small campfires. Our food service was on individual metal gear which each soldier had in his duffel bag. After eating, a metal barrel was filled with water which we used to boil water and throw in the food service equipment in a vain attempt to kill what bacteria accumulated. I developed a severe gum infection but was not able to leave my central post, having no second in command. Luckily, there was a village nearby with a German dentist. I visited him, and he told me that if I could get him some wound packs that we wore on our ammunition belts, he could treat my infection. Wound packs were available, and the dentist was correct. I still have my teeth.

It appeared that the mission was accomplishing nothing, so we returned to Giessen and found that nothing had changed. My wife had a University of Chicago education, but she had no food preparation training. In honor of my return, she had acquired some veal chops in the local market and, using a massive Army cookbook, tried to cook them. I found them inedible. Josie, the dog, which had been hauled up to the top on the rope of the pole in Darmstadt and was barking and squealing all night while I was on duty in the open, didn't like the veal chops either. I had sharp pains at the table, which I attributed to my recent Mannheim visit, and thought that the pain was due to food poison which the German dentist didn't quite wipe out. Giessen had a medical clinic set up recently in an occupied German hospital, and I went there to get rid of the pain.

The hospital had been occupied by medics, and they had an opening cocktail party going on full blast when I arrived. There was a medic on duty, and his examination of me revealed an enlarged appendix, which he thought was about to burst. He brought in one of the officers who was unhappy to leave the party, and he confirmed the diagnosis. I was the hospital's first patient, so he called in a number of other officers to witness the first operation. The medic who had first examined me stated—true or not—that this would be his first operation. I didn't feel that I was a guinea pig, but felt honored to have so many witnesses. I remember that the anesthetics I was administered allowed me to walk after the operation, assisted down the hall to a vacant room with a cot. No gurneys were available at that moment.

I was awakened early the next morning by my company's first sergeant and a private who had been assigned to duty the night before to guard the fleet of trucks that we were using. The private decided that the best place to watch the trucks was on the roof of one of the garages we were using for repairs. He had brought up onto the roof a kerosene stove which he was using to stay warm. The first sergeant noticed this and ordered him to get it off the roof immediately. In his haste to do that, he spilled kerosene on the roof—which caught fire, and the building burned. We were lucky that he was not injured and there was only one tractor in the garage at the time. I was not supposed to be out of the medical clinic, but there was no choice. I left after two days. I requested a medical leave to travel to Lugano where the weather was much warmer. The request was granted. Zelda was a great nurse, and I recovered quickly. The damaged tractor had been repaired to usable condition in my absence.

After my return to Giessen, Colonel McAfee asked me what I wanted to do in the Army. I responded that I was disappointed not be able to discover whether arms were coming out of Mannheim Depot and that I might discover that if I went to Israel, which was just finished with the 1948 war in which they had roundly beaten five Arab armies. I was able to suggest this since I knew that my father had business interests overseas, and he had participated with another entrepreneur in forming a company known as Israeli Electric Products. The company was run by Maurice Bassan, a graduate of L'Ecole Polytechnique, the French military academy. Bassan might know since he was a former advisor to the King of Jordan and a participant in the Syrian battles that France was involved in. In one of the battles, Moshe Dayan was struck in the eye with a bullet. He recovered but had to wear an eye patch after that. McAfee contacted Washington, and in a few days, I was put into detached service and allowed to go to Israel with Zelda.

Civilian clothes had to be made up from material purchased in our local Post Exchange and tailored by a civilian tailor. I was issued a new civilian passport indicating that I was a businessman and interested in buying an Israeli product: oranges. I was twenty-two years old at the time, and I am sure that even in civilian clothes, I did not look like a buyer of anything. El Al was the name of the new airline that took us there. We were its sole passengers. The pilots were from Ireland and loquacious about hating the British.

When we landed at Lydda Airport, we were greeted by two Israeli officers—Ezer Weitzman and Moshe Dayan. Dayan took an immediately liking to Zelda, my strikingly attractive twenty-one-year-old wife. Weitzman took me into a nearby hangar to meet with a person who knew me well. Sitting at a desk dressed in civilian clothes was my former tactical officer, Major Brady, who was in charge of G-2 Company at West Point. His only comment to me was to take all the pictures that I could. He would get them from me when I left two weeks later. In the meantime, we would be Col. Bassan's houseguests in Jerusalem and travel the country in Israeli Army transportation.

I had always wanted to visit Israel based on my early religious education in Hebrew School and at Wyoming Seminary. Israel was a brand-new nation when Zelda and I arrived on my detached service visit. I have to admit that I was never so religious to believe many of the biblical stories; however, I was in awe as to how the Israelis beat five stronger Arab armies at once and anxious to learn how they did it. Dayan had a cocktail party for Zelda at his residence and introduced us to much of the Army brass. I felt honored to have that kind of attention paid to us. After all, I was a lieutenant, and all the people I met were field grade or above. Dayan invited me to witness a paratroop training jump the next night. I was not impressed with it. I could tell that he was not either. He certainly didn't learn how to fall properly. According to Charlie Weiss (no relative, but night editor of the *Jerusalem Post*), Dayan broke his leg jumping out of a second-story window when the husband of the wife he had been in bed with came home unexpectedly. Zelda was fascinated with many of the ancient artifacts Dayan had captured, and she made a note to visit him at his store in the Dan Hotel in Haifa when he set up shop. Years later on a return trip to Israel, we purchased some of the artifacts from him. Colonel Bassan took me on a tour of the Jerusalem front on which he had to capture a hill in order to make it Israel's capital city. Furthermore, many thousands of Jews lived there and their descendants had lived there without a break for thousands of years. His problem was to take it in a frontal assault. Looking at the terrain, I suggested that a flanking movement would have been much less costly. He pointed out that he had no control since he had no contact with most of his non-uniformed soldiers. They spoke many different languages, and had few weapons past the first two rows. He estimated that the Jordanian defenders had a limited amount of ammunition and that after they had killed off his forward attackers, the ones in the rear would pick up the dropped weapons and continue. The loss of Israeli attackers was horrific, but the frontal charge worked. The Jordanian soldiers that were left in their trench had been shackled to their posts and were not supported by other Jordanians who fled to the rear. The capture of that hill allowed what forces he had left to enter the center of Jerusalem, a line was drawn in establishing a truce.

We left the hill and walked up to a building in the neighborhood which was literally cut in half by the negotiated truce line. A guard from each side was stationed on their side of the line. The two guards could not have been more than twenty feet apart. They had loaded rifles, and I observed that the safeties were off. The Israeli guard was carrying a German weapon, and the Jordanian a British one. I asked Bassan whether I could examine the Israeli soldier's gun, and he permitted me to do so after he drew his pistol. All official German weapons have identification. This one was clearly visible. I made a mental note of the number. We left the building and, on the way back to Bassan's apartment, stopped at a toilet room where I used the latrine. I wrote the serial number on the underside of my shoe's sole lining and left it there for further reference. I was not convinced that weapons had come from Mannheim. The Russians had captured mountains of German weapons, and I wanted to show that at least this weapon wasn't a Mannheim one. Much later, it turned out that it might have been. The Germans were meticulous in identifying their weapons using a process of numbering them. The number was in the Mannheim group, but there was no way anyone would know whether it was part of the Russian arms captured by the Germans. Russia, having been the first nation to recognize Israel as a country, allowed cargo airplanes to utilize a temporary airfield in Czechoslovakia and was presumed to have sold used weapons to most anyone who wanted them. I had obtained some of the information I was looking for, but it was flimsy evidence.

Zelda and I had been flown to Eilat in an Israeli military

transport. At that time, Eilat, then a sandy beach adjacent to Jordan was fortified by Israeli troops. It was a particularly hot day, and the only structure standing was a tent. The commanding officer declared that the troops could have the balance of the day off and go swimming if Zelda would go with them. There were no women on the post, and she was a pretty twenty-one-year-old in a bathing suit. She must have looked like manna from heaven. She said that she enjoyed the attention. The base commander enlightened me as to how they planned to build up Eilat and turn it into a seaport. Looking at it then, it was hard to envision—but it did happen.

We were returned to the airport and traveled to Haifa and checked into the Dan Hotel beautifully sited on a hill overlooking the Haifa Harbor. After we returned for the night, the phone rang. A lady's voice with a decidedly American accent said that I was to meet her at the hotel bus stop at 6:00 a.m. and she would give me some information I would like to have. At the bus stop the next morning was a very good-looking lady with her left hand wearing a ring that looked like a miniature ring that cadets and midshipmen give their fiancées. I thought that I knew her, but when I said hello, she said, "Don't talk to me. Sit several rows behind me on the bus, and don't get off until I do. Then follow me." I followed her directions. The bus went into the harbor warehouse area. I was struck by an architect's nameplate on one of the warehouse buildings—Ed Allen. This was an architect from Wilkes-Barre, Pennsylvania, and I knew him. Thinking about this coincidence, I followed the lady into another nearby warehouse. When we were inside the building, she turned and said to me, "We met at a West Point hop in 1946. I decided to marry a navy man instead of the cadet I was dating at the time. I thought you'd like to meet him." We went upstairs to an office.

She introduced me to her husband, Paul Schulman, and that was the last I saw of her.

Paul Schulman was wearing an Israeli Army uniform. He said that he was the chief commanding officer of the Israeli Navy. As a member of the West Point class of '46, I felt awkward since I had not obtained high rank as had the man I was visiting. He stated that he had left the navy and was told to meet me while in Israel. It needed foreign training officers to whip the Israeli army into shape. He graduated from Annapolis. Both he and his roommate elected to go into the submarine service. The British had turned over all their military equipment when they left Israel to the Arab armies. One of the pieces of the equipment was the Battleship *Bristol*, a German battleship captured by the British (then the world's largest battleship, captured intact in Argentina). The British named it *The King Farouk* and turned it over to the Egyptians with a British training crew. The ship had been berthed in Alexandria but was moved offshore to Tel Aviv preparatory to shelling the city. Schulman was sent to Italy to pick up a four-man submarine. Schulman took the electrically powered submarine to the *Farouk* with an assistant and attached explosive charges on critical spots on the hull. He set the timed explosive charges. The ship blew up. The Egyptian Navy surrounding the battleship was so frightened about this display of military power that all Egyptian ships went back to Alexandria and never came back.

I told him it was a shame that no one in the news knew about it. He laughed and said that when he returned to his Haifa apartment, there was a telegram under the door. It had one word—"congratulations"—and it was signed by his Annapolis roommate who was in Naval Intelligence.

The remainder of our Israeli trip was fascinating. It became obvious to me that President Truman had decided to take over supporting Israel to establish an American presence in the Middle East, which we never had. On the other hand, many of the Arab military figured we were establishing a base there and they wanted it removed. They still do to this day.

Bassan's daughter's wedding, to which we had been invited, was interesting. Food was rare so that an after-wedding party could not be successful unless it was provided. Colonel Bassan had me accompany him in his car to the town of Metulah and crossed over the border into Lebanon on a road without any border controls. He knew this area because he had served there in the French army. We drove to a farm not far away, and he purchased chickens and a car full of other food to be used in the party. The transaction went smoothly. The local Arabs were quite friendly to Bassan.

Back in Jerusalem at the wedding, the procedure was as if there were no hostilities and genuine joyfulness at the ceremony. I was surprised both by the fact that I hated the suit I had brought, which did not go too well and was too hot, and the food and beverages which tasted wonderful after ten days of too little food because of the rationing. I met the bride's younger brother, Raffe, who was to become an airplane mechanic when he was older. He died mysteriously, apparently from poison, when he was working on an Israeli modification of a Myster's wing. The aircraft industry was nonexistent there, but became big later on and still is. I could tell even then that the small factories manufacturing planes then would probably become a major industry. It did to the extent that Israel is now one of the world's principal suppliers of parts in the industry.

We returned to Germany on El Al. I had been silently relieved of my pictures. When we returned, we went to the officers' mess before going to our apartment and had a large meal. We both had lost weight and tried to make up for it.

Giessen was our major depot in the American zone, and I felt that I could use depot training there. My branch still was desperate for training officers. It wanted me and used me in that capacity for about six months when I transferred to Munich.

Before leaving Giessen to move to Munich, Zelda and I took several trips. The first was to visit Bernie Janis in Munich and meet his new fiancée. I also wanted to see what the city looked like and where we were to live. Bernie's lady friend and he had met in Bad Tolz, First Division Headquarters, where he was the Division General's Aide. Gerda Knoche was her name, and she had been a schoolteacher and a Nazi Party officer. She had been teaching German children in Poland and fled with the Nazi officials from Warsaw when the German troops were fleeing the country to go to Bavaria where Hitler had invited loyal party members to go as a last resort. Physically, she was skinny as a rail, but Bernie told me that she was the girl he wanted to marry. I told Bernie that he was nuts to take on this burden, but if the wedding went through, I would support him against the objections that the Army might have. I also warned him that he would probably lose his job as Aide to the General since the ban on living with Nazi women was still in effect. I was unfortunately correct. The General fired him and transferred him to Berlin where he was put in charge of furniture distribution for Army quarters—a nothing job.

Bill Richards, a classmate, told me that the procurement office in Paris, to which he had been assigned, gave him little to do and he found it difficult to live there because of high living costs. Zelda and I had been assigned to Munich. Zelda and I could use the trains without charge, and we used an overnight one to Paris. When we arrived, Bill and his wife Joan were there to meet us. He suggested that he would consider swapping cities with me—as if we had any possibility to do that. His wife Joan liked it there, and we spent a pleasant day. Walking up the Champs-Elysees toward the Arc de Triomphe in the early evening, our two wives fell behind us by about one block looking in the store windows while Bill and I were engaged in conversation. He noticed that they were missing and we turned around to see them waving their arms and screaming. There were two dark men looking like Arabs, holding knives against their backs. We had no weapons, but we both had heavy buckle belts, which we stripped off and ran as fast as we could toward them. Luckily, a gendarme appeared up the street and the two knifemen ran away and disappeared. Bill's comment was that it was a shame the gendarme came into view. I felt differently. Joan was noticeably pregnant and, if there was to be contact, might have been seriously injured.

We took a trip to the city of Zeist in Holland. Coming over from America on the *Queen Mary*, my mother met a Dutch couple by the name of Van Kempen. They were silver manufacturers and sold their products in their stores in the Dutch colonies, primarily the Caribbean. My mother told them that I was about to be married to Zelda (who was with them) and suggested that we meet them at their Holland residence, bringing them food products since the food in Holland was still being rationed. I received a telephone call from the Van Kempens and made a date to visit them. We bought a large box of groceries and took it with us to Zeist.

When we arrived at the castle—which was, to my surprise, their residence—we were met by their servants who treated us like royalty. We learned in later conversations that they were cousins to the king, and they had a son by the name of Anton who was joining us for dinner. Anton and I were the same age. When he looked at Zelda, he had tears in his eyes. His father said that the girl who lived down the road was Jewish, and Zelda resembled her strongly. It apparently was a love affair which was ruined since she was pulled out of her house one night by German troops, raped, and brutally killed—with her naked corpse thrown on her porch for the neighborhood to see.

Anton guessed that German officers would take over the castle as a residence. There was a crawl space over the living room ceiling where Anton could lie and hear the officers' conversation. The family had a tunnel running from the rear basement wall to the waste area, with a path to the sea where garbage boats would pick up the trash. Anton had a small sailboat there, which he used for fishing. He used it at night to convey to British Intelligence the entire conversation he heard from the Nazi officers during the occupation. He also buried much of the silver inventory that the family had on hand. I received word from my mother that she had received—in Kingston, Pennsylvania—a large box with a few beautiful silver dining room pieces addressed to us with a card saying that it was for the food we brought them.

When we returned to Giessen, we packed up our Dodge with all our possessions. We had plenty of room to spare and drove to 177 Gruenwalder Strasse in Munich. It was the second and third floor of a duplex house building. It was located near a corner bus stop next door to a grocery store. The location was in the Harlaching section of town and a direct line on the streetcar (free passage for military) to my office in the central city. It was a short walk from our house to the zoo and Municipal Park next to it.

My office was at 9 Possart Strasse, in Munich. It was a six-story building one block away from the Opera. There were two offices in the building: the procurement office and Radio Free Europe on the top floor. Our mission was to purchase from German reparations such materials as the U.S. Government wanted. This was not military supplies when I first located there. It became a purchasing office for use to buy miscellaneous US gov't. supplies.

We purchased china used at our embassies, the furniture used in our barracks and officers' quarters, food supplies, and all sorts of equipment. The elevator was geared to stop at our floor for foreigners who needed to reach Radio Free Europe, Russians and Poles went there, and I wondered whether the station was for pure propaganda dissemination or part of military intelligence.

The OSS was closing down and the CIA being formed but not yet, to our knowledge, operational. The first floor was empty. I was solicited by a number of very attractive women who offered their sexual services in exchange for the use of those offices. Fortunately, having been just married months before, I never allowed them in.

Our officer in charge was Captain Ernest DeBlois. He was a sergeant with a brevet commission of captain. He had been in the Army since the sinking of the Panay in China, and retained an amazing amount of knowledge of the procurement system. I could not have had a better teacher.

The war in Korea had broken out and the First Division had been moved from Germany, I assumed that I would be moved to the Pacific in the near future. Captain Deblois suggested that I prepare to leave Germany. He was training an American national who had grown up in Berlin and spoke perfect German. He said that his name was Henry Berliner. He had somehow escaped from the Nazis in the 1930s and moved to New York. He had not been accepted for military service, but volunteered to join the Intelligence Services which were smaller than normal after the war's end. Some civilians were sent overseas to fill in positions which were open. He was one of them.

I was delighted to learn that his father was an employee of an American company's German operations. This made him familiar with some of the people with whom we would need to deal with. He needed a car, and since I was preparing to leave I

sold him Zelda's Fiat. We expected to take our Dodge back to
the States with us. We were offered a price from the owner of a
German service station which was greater than I thought I could
realize in the States for it. However, we needed a car until our
departure date which I felt would be soon. He agreed to delay
taking possession of it for up to one month. We decided to take
some short trips to utilize the free time that we had, but also
decided to buy a European car for a lesser price than we had
already received to bring home.

Special Services had arranged for package trips to various
places. We picked out one to North Africa which I particularly
wanted to see at the point where our invading troops encountered
the French under De Gaulle and later the Germans under
Rommel. The trip was ten days off. In the meantime, I shopped
for a French or British auto and took a trip to Paris on the night
train. Bill Richards suggested that I visit a British office which
representatives of British manufacturers had established in Paris.
I did so. While sitting in the waiting room to see a representative
I struck up a conversation with a British salesman from the
Hillman Company who was there to object to the French refusal
to allow one of the cars he had brought in to be allowed into
France since it had body damage of the type requiring factory
repairs. I asked to see the pictures of the damage and whether
he could call the factory to see how long it would take to replace
the panels which needed it. He called his office from the waiting
room and told me that since they had the parts in stock it could
be done in one day. I told him that I would be happy to buy the
car if he would drive me down to the docks where the car was
being held providing that I could buy it at half price.

The car had not yet gone through customs and could be
driven in its condition to the factory in England which was in a
London commercial section. His company agreed to my offer. I

had the car moved on to the ferry which was soon to return to England. The car attracted a lot of attention driving it from the dock to the factory which I reached after dark but which still had an office open. One of the employees drove me to a hotel. When I contacted Zelda to inform her that we now owned a British car she seemed quite happy about it. The repairs were made the next day and I left the country on the first ferry available which was due to land in France but because of poor weather landed in Belgium. Taking it into Belgium was no problem. I did not bring it into France since I guessed that the French might claim an import tax. It had first been on French land. I drove directly to Munich.

The car worked perfectly. We drove it to Zurich without incident on our first stop for our scheduled African visit. We had dinner with Bennie Guggenheim at the Bauer Au Lac Hotel. We had met him previously on one of our Swiss weekend visits and had become socially friendly with him. I told him that he must be a lowly organizational member of the world's largest gold mine operations, but he was still working. His family had bought the Hearst gold mines and added them to their other assets. He said that if I worked hard enough to please my superiors, I might become a captain. I responded that my great grandmother had already promoted me to General Nuisance, and I was about to become a captain.

When we returned to our room, there was a telegram at the door. I opened it and read that I was to report to Battalion Headquarters Monday morning. It was Friday night. I could make it, leaving Zelda at our residence on the way. The African trip was canceled. It was twenty years until I caught a glimpse of Africa.

The remaining days in Munich were occupied by office matters which were much heavier than usual since Captain Ernie

Dublois, the military office manager, had been assigned to pick up Von Braun's Nazi employees who were in Russian captivity. This required a trip to Warsaw which he volunteered to take since I was considered by the Russians to be an enemy of their State, and they said it in their radio broadcasts. This was during the Berlin boycott to Americans. Truman cured this successfully with the airlift. Jimmie was born in a hospital taken over by our army and run by nuns. Zelda had complications requiring transfusions of blood which in later life was a contributing cause of her inability to obtain proper blood matches. We paid little attention to that because she appeared to be in excellent health. Her mother had come to visit us a week or two before Jimmy's birth. I was attending a compulsory officer's call when it occurred. We agreed to name him Robert, but Zelda's mother, Anna Klein, decided that she like James better and filled out the papers accordingly. I wasn't there to object.

She asked me to gather nine Jewish men and a "Mohl" to conduct the circumcision. My office at 9 Possart Strasse was located near an alley that ran into Possart Strasse, I had never visited it since I considered it a dangerous neighborhood. I walked into Mohlstrasse and was surprised to find myself in a bustling black market. Fortunately, my German had improved enough by that time to inform the merchant in the first stall the purpose of my visit. He directed me to a building down the street where a large meeting was being held. I walked into what appeared to be a trial, a Jewish Beit Din, with a raised platform in a good-sized hall and about a hundred people in attendance. One of the spectators told me that this was a Beit Din—a civil trial. The platform had a Rabbi on it who was performing his duties as a judge. One of the trial participants paid him what appeared to be a large sum of some currency which the judge turned over to the other of the parties. I knew that German courts were in existence but I also knew that these people were refugees from Poland and Russia who would never set foot in a German court. They had their own form of justice which was rigidly observed.

When the trial was finished and the spectators were leaving the room I went over to the Rabbi and explained what I wanted in German. He answered me in perfect English and told me to come back the next morning at 10:00 a.m. in time for the ceremony. My automobile was the large Dodge sedan I had shipped to Germany two years earlier. When I arrived to pick up the "volunteers" they had a Mohl and eight people and they all climbed on top of each other into the car. I felt like a driver of a car in the circus where loads of people—clowns—come out. The springs held up. I'll never know how, but we did arrive at my apartment safely. My mother-in-law had prepared delicacies which the group devoured. They must have been half starved. The circumcision took place without a hitch (Jimmie fathered two children, so the operation must have been successful.)

I returned the group to Mohl Strasse in three shifts to save the auto springs and for safety purposes through Munich streets. Jimmie was raised as an infant by a Bavarian lady named Ursula who stayed with us for the next few years. We sent for her when we returned to the United States. She eventually married and left our employ when Jimmie was about four years old. Josie, my dog from Darmstadt, was his companion. Jimmy had a mysterious person in his mind that did not leave him until well after he was back in the United States.

I reported on Monday morning at Battalion headquarters to the General in charge of the Zone. He was there along with the Quartermaster. Danny Graham was also there. I was given a date that I was to leave for the States. I was told that I was to be troop commander of the ship on which we would return. Danny was to be in charge of a group of prisoners we were bringing back to the States. The prisoners were top secret and not allowed to talk to anyone on the boat. As troop commander, I was to assign duties to all officers including a General who was retiring. I was assigned the troop commander's cabin and all the perks of the commanding officer. I was still a lieutenant, as was Danny. I could not figure out why he apparently had been assigned to what was an inferior position with his quarters adjacent to the prisoners. I was given a few days to pack our possessions and ship them from Munich by military transport to the boat.

The boat trip was totally different than the one I had coming from Germany to the States. Our car was picked up at the train station, and we had an overnight cabin on the train. The accommodations were to our minds first class on the ship. I assigned the General to take care of Jimmy, then two years old, at his suggestion. I walked around the ship constantly to make sure that none of the prisoners were loose. Danny told me that one had escaped but he was sure that he would find him. He did in a lifeboat where he was sleeping. The trip involved boat drills at which Jimmy took offense. The noise of the horns during the drills disturbed his ears and he outshouted them. We had his hair cut by the ship's barber so that he would look presentable on arrival in Brooklyn. The trip took more than a week because of the weather. When we arrived, my parents were at the Brooklyn dock.

I had a packet handcuffed to my left arm by a ship's officer who gave me a slip of paper with an East Sixteenth Street address and told me to go directly to the office by using waiting cab. I felt like a Brink's messenger and requested a pistol. He refused, saying that it would make me conspicuous—as if I wasn't already with the packet on my arm, parachute boots, and wings on my chest.

I hadn't time to meet my parents, but I could see that they

were waving to Zelda and Jimmie on the rail of the boat. I left and was driving under the tunnel to the west side of Manhattan. I asked the driver why we were going to the west side when the address of the destination was on the east side. He said that since it was St. Patrick's Day there was a parade and the address was too close to Washington Square. He said that he felt that he could not turn back in the street on which he would deliver me since it was one-way and he could not get through the parade. I felt that walking through Washington Square with the bag that strongly resembled a bank delivery bag was not a safe thing to do, but I left the cab after several minutes of looking to see whether the park was deserted. It appeared to be, so I left the cab, running across it to well past George Washington's statue in the middle in its center to within a hundred feet of the crowd. I felt an object in my back. I turned to discover what appeared to be a .45-caliber pistol pressed into it and a civilian black man holding it. He said, "I want your bag." I replied, "You'll have to cut off my arm to get it, and if you do, there's a policeman less than a hundred feet away that can hear me whether you use the pistol or a knife. Do you feel like spending the rest of your life in prison or ending it in the electric chair?" The would-be thief cursed and turned and ran back across the park.

I told the policeman of the incident. He took me through the crowd and parade to the other side. He apparently was experienced but did not comment that it was an unusual crime to attempt. The comment from the military officer I reached in the receiving office was "This is New York. What do you expect?" I found a cab outside in the next block and returned to the boat in less than half the time it took to reach the office. My folks and my wife hardly missed me. I was told that my car and other contents would not be available until the next day. I could receive a phone call when it was ready and come to New York to retrieve it. We drove to Wilkes-Barre stopping on route at the first Howard Johnsons for lunch.

I wondered what had happened to the "prisoners." I did not realize that we were delivering the engineers Von Braun needed to solve the problems we were having with our fighter jets and the start of the rocket program. I understood why Deblois had gone to Warsaw to pay for them and bring them to Bremerhaven. Why I wasn't given this information is a matter of conjecture, but the fact that Danny was shifting his branch to military intelligence was not known to me at that time. The facts were that a taxi was waiting for me at the boat in Brooklyn. My request for a pistol to make a delivery of documents had been denied. The route that the driver used had possibly been timed to meet someone in the park on the West Side since my return route to the boat took less than half the time we used to get there. I saw no one in the park which had unobstructed views to the other side when I left the cab the driver of which had been paid to take me there. I had run through the park to make up for lost time in the delivery of the papers. The threatening gunman had a .45, which was not the kind of pistol I would expect an ordinary thief to carry unless he was military. All of this made me wonder whether I had been set up for a robbery which would have taken place had I not run almost to the other side, and I am a pretty good runner. The assignment I received next continued to bother me. I went to my parents' home in Pennsylvania and took the bus back to New York where I received what seemed to me to be strange orders.

Our office secretary was a pretty young woman I realized that she probably had a way to enter the file cabinet. I persuaded her to let me look at the documents when Archie was not present. I was surprised to see that Forrestal had concluded a deal with Time Oil Company, but the document we had was not signed. Since Time Oil appeared to have no assets to speak of, I assumed that it was an arm of Lehman Brothers. I took my suspicions to General Hayden who directed me to the Inspector General. It was at this time that I received a telephone call from Louis Smith—the director of the Jewish Community Center in Wilkes-Barre, Pennsylvania—saying that an army officer had just left his office asking him questions about me and my family background. A few days later, I was required to sign a top secret nondisclosure document whereby I would not state anything to anyone about my activities in the army. That included procurement. I could not determine whether the top secret document was to protect the army, which had gone along with MacArthur's attempt to set up an expeditionary force to take over the Chinese oil depot, or whether it had something to do with the Forrestal case. In any case, somebody wanted my mouth shut. I signed the document. I went to see Bill Reed. I asked Bill whether I was in trouble without revealing the top secret clearance. He had contacts with high brass both at Lehman Bros. and the Secretary of Defense. He asked me to see him in his office a few days later. I did. His message was a simple one: "Don't go down to the docks." When I asked him why, he responded, "Industrial accidents happen all the time. I would hate to have you suffer one." I said that my duties might very well require me to go there since all oil came over or through the docks. He said, "Leave the army." I decided to offer my resignation.

I submitted my resignation, but it was denied. I saw the Inspector General again and requested to learn how to leave the Army. He told me that a regular commission could always be requested to be turned into a reserve commission. A reservist on active duty could be called into the service at any time. However, the army had implemented a policy of allowing reservists with over forty months of overseas duty to request discharge. I had forty months and two days. I received notice of discharge permission the same day I received orders to report to Texas to operate the largest ROTC group in the country. It was being run by a Lt. Colonel and offered a potential eventual promotion along with the opportunity to complete my legal training at the University of Texas Law School. Having completed a year and a half of law school at night at Loyola Law School of Los Angeles, this was a hard offer to refuse. I needed a way to make a living when I left the army. But I remembered Bill Reed's advice and acted on it.

A month or two later when I was selling shoes in the warehouse of Triangle Shoe Store, a Colonel came in and interviewed me about the Forrestal Case. He also insisted that I report to the Tobyhanna Depot where I would become an S-3 (training officer) with the possible raise in the rank to Major. I thought that my uniform in my casket would look better with major's leaves rather than Captain's, but I turned him down. My discharge papers did not arrive until more than a year later. I feel that but for Bill Reed, I would not be alive today.

In February of 1951, I was assigned to return to New York. This ended our European tour of forty months and two days.

The trip to New York was long but very interesting. After my greeting on Union Square in Manhattan by some black would-be thief with a pistol, I believed that whatever I was assigned to would not be pleasant. I was wrong again in my personal predictions. The Triangle Shoe Company had leased an apartment at the southeast corner of Central Park West and West Ninety-Sixth Street. It was an ideal location for Zelda, Jimmie, Josie, and me. The subway entrance was across the street and parking was permitted on many of the streets in the area. However, it was so difficult to find free spaces that I parked my car on the west side of the Hudson under a bridge near a subway station easily reachable from our temporary home. Zelda loved the location since there was a playground across the street in

Central Park, and it was clearly visible from our rooms. Jimmy apparently liked it also. We sent Josie to Kingston after a while since she required frequent outdoor dog latrines. I met a Swiss skier in his convertible auto driving through the park who I knew from skiing in Austria. He brought me up-to-date as to what was happening in Europe particularly with regard to postwar construction of the 40 percent of German cities destroyed by General Curtis Lemay's bombers. I was amazed at the progress even though I had just returned from Germany. My father was very generous in letting us use the company apartment for the months I was stationed in the city.

My military purpose was to become educated to run an oil depot. The classes were held at Caven Point, New Jersey, the locale of the First World War's Black Tom explosion. Civilian clothes were the rule, and transportation was public. I noticed Chinese characters in the margins of the depot plans we were studying, but had no idea where the actual depot was. New York has a large Chinatown and I assumed that the printer was in that area. Our class consisted of six officers, one of whom, Bobby Land, dropped out early in our studies. He was West Point's wrestling star having won the national collegiate championship. I was a bit disturbed by this since I figured that with his muscle, wherever we were going it might come in handy. We were all qualified paratroopers, but that was the only common thread. That signified to me that we would be dropped into an assigned oil depot. We were studying an oil distribution plant, which probably could only be reached from the air. After a few weeks we were assigned to different oil companies in New York City.

My oil company was Standard Oil of New York located on the south side of Manhattan across from the fish market and Kelly's bar. Our lunch consisted of two martinis for my instructor and a Coca Cola for me. I never understood how he held his liquor.

He appeared perfectly sober at all times. He introduced me to his organization's employees one of whom was Mr. Levy in charge of exploration. Since I had been to Israel not too many months before, I asked him if there was any oil producing potential there. His answer was that there were stratigraphic traps in the Sinai Peninsula, but with the huge discoveries in Saudi Arabia there was little likelihood of Socony drilling there since the Arabian oil would be cheaper and easier to produce. His comments stuck in my mind as I read about new oil strikes in Arabia and the formation of Aramco.

My instructor drove us to one of Socony's producing wells in western Pennsylvania, the collection area of the Pennsylvania crude. There were numerous miniature drilling rigs operating with hand pump gas stations. They had cardboard signs advertising the price per gallon of locally produced gasoline. The farm owners would drill their own wells and distill the crude, burn off the gas, and sell the tar base to road contractors. The gasoline had no additives so the octane rating was quite low and varied from pump to pump. Ford developed a timer-changing device, mounted it on the dashboard of their Model Ts, and the car owner could use the cheap gas. The instructor stated that this could be utilized on military vehicles, but the modification could probably not be done in the field. It was a revelation to me that we could adapt our engines to any octane of gasoline we acquired in the field. This made the cost and ability to get our vehicles moving on foreign territory less prohibitive.

After the road trip, I was once more assigned to New York and instructed to get back in uniform. We were shocked to discover that Truman had fired MacArthur and assigned General Westmoreland to take over in Korea. We were held in New York for a short time, and I was privileged to witness the ticker-tape parade held for MacArthur. Orders were received to report to

Fort MacArthur in San Pedro, California. We were assigned a week to get there.

Zelda and I decided to drive there, leaving Jimmie with her mother in Wilkes-Barre. I traded in my Hillman Minx for a new Buick, and we drove out stopping only to sleep, eat, and visit Jack Shuman in Rolla, Missouri, on the way back. Jack was my closest friend and best man at our wedding.

I had a week to report to Fort MacArthur in San Pedro, a short distance south of Los Angeles. Jimmy would stay with Zelda's parent, and Zelda and I would drive across the country stopping in Rolla, Missouri, to visit Jack Schuman. We were fortunate that we had no major problems with our car and made excellent time on the road. We found Jack quickly since he was well known in Rolla where his ancestors had been among the original settlers. The following generations had never sold the land, having leased it to builders who paid rent for the acreage they used. Fort Leonard Wood was not far away. The family owned a commercial laundry which had a contract to do the laundry for the Post. I assumed that was the reason Jack selected Quartermaster as his branch.

We stayed overnight. Zelda and I were impressed by the large amount of Meissen China on display in all rooms. He had several barrels of it still wrapped in the containers. He said that he had collected the china during the period the Russians closed Berlin to our being able to supply it with food. His uncle was president of the Union Carbide Corporation, which had its own planes. Jack asked him to get permission to fly in food and send the empty planes back with the china he accumulated. I asked him whether he had any guilt feelings about it. He said not at all. He was convinced that it was stolen by the Nazis throughout Eastern Europe from their occupied territories. He had called me at my office in Munich during that period to say that one of his jobs was to meet the planes of American officials and take them around Berlin. I remembered that he had called me to ask about a congressman from Pennsylvania by the name of Dan Flood who had just landed. His large suitcase had fallen off the stairwell ramp, and the items in the bag were lying on the ground. Jack questioned his validity as a Congressman and was given my name to confirm that he was legitimate. I told Jack that he was a family friend and to put him on the phone to recognize his voice. It was Dan, all right. He said that he would stop to see me in Munich on the way home. He did. I told Jack that Dan was on the Military Affairs Committee, and Jack had better treat him with courtesy if he ever wanted to be a general.

Jack decided that he would like to ride with us on part of our trip west. He had resigned from the Army and was bored with the job he had at the laundry. He went with us as far as Steamboat Springs in Colorado where Zelda had taken her acting training after college. He wanted to see the Face on the Bar room floor which uncannily Zelda resembled in spite of the worn-out paint still there. He left us there and returned to Rolla by bus. I didn't see him again until our tenth West Point reunion, where he told me that he had Parkinson's disease and might not be back for a fifteenth. His father had died from the disease at a very young age. Apparently, it was genetic in his family. He passed away a few years later in a hospital in St. Louis.

We continued our trip to Los Angeles, arriving there in the evening. When we arrived in Westwood, the Los Angeles suburb in which my uncle Charlie Koff resided with his wife Ann, we went to Charlie's house directly. Ann came out of her front door and looked awful. She said that she was embarrassed to see us in her condition, but there was no food in the house she could offer us. We took her to a nearby grocery and brought her whatever she needed. She explained that Charlie had moved to their garage, which was detached from the house, and had put in a second floor with furniture and a piano where he did his work arranging music. He had started in the business of rack jobbing hosiery in neighborhood grocery stores and was on the road most of the day supplying merchandise. When he came home, he would go directly to his piano and continue his arranging work. He had left her without money for days. She had no car to get food if she had none. He was apparently so pressured by his two jobs that he had not thought to even come into the house. We waited for him to come home, and I told him that he might get a third job—in jail for nonsupport. I don't believe that he liked our visit.

Charlie was getting his rack merchandise from Triangle Shoe Company suppliers. We threatened to convey his state of affairs to the company, which would have endangered his business. I told him that unless he procured a car for Ann and gave her enough money to live on, he would be in worse financial shape than he appeared to be in at the moment. He agreed to do that but insisted that I take a day off and accompany him on a round of his stores so that I could see what he was doing. I agreed to do this but had to postpone the date to one when I could get away from Fort MacArthur. I had not yet checked in. We left him and proceeded to report into the post at San Pedro.

When we arrived at the base, I was taken to the commanding General's office. I was delighted to meet General Hayden—who was a Colonel when I last saw him at West Point. He was in charge of Coast Artillery Training. Coast Artillery was not too important then because rocket propelled missiles and aircraft made it obsolete. However, the base at San Pedro was used as the point from which the shipping of petroleum supplies to Korea from Long Beach had been designated. General Hayden and I had met on a training mission for my West Point class shooting 90-mm guns at air targets. It was near Savannah for antiaircraft training. He had requested that I be assigned to him because he needed a petroleum officer. Willie Bigler, a classmate, had the job but wished to get into action while Korea was still a war zone. His decision to go was fortuitous. He became a General in a relatively short time.

Unfortunately, the Post had no quarters available for a married Captain, which I had become. The allowance for lodgings was not high, and we had to look around for an apartment we could afford. We decided to move to Venice which had low priced apartments and was fairly close to Charlie's house in Westwood. We signed a one year lease in the Lincoln Apartments. They were not comfortable. We looked for areas closer to my office and decided to move to Lakewood, a new suburb closer to Fort MacArthur at the north edge of Long Beach. We signed up for a house to be delivered about six months to a year later which was fine since we wanted to wait until our lease expired. We were among the first few residents of a five hundred–house development, which allowed us to pick our location near to the twelfth hole of the Douglas Aircraft's golf course. The course was for Douglas employees, but active military could use it without charge.

Zelda loved the house which had cost us $10,800 ($200 down and 4 percent mortgage, less expensive than our apartment rent). The lot size was 50' x 100' and the house came with a nice front and rear garden and one-car garage. The climate was very favorable. We did not need air-conditioning. Our heating unit was a floor-mounted gas heater in the center of the house, which worked very well. We had a back porch where we could overlook our country domain. It had become our living room, day or night.

Zelda had always like gardening and discovered that she could get a free gardening class at Long Beach City College.

Tuition and books were free. The first two years of college were paid for by the oil revenues paid to the State by the oil companies. As a result, I was required to put in a different kind of grass in our lawns and build a brick plant enclosure in front of the house. It was a good idea because all the houses were so similar, it was hard to distinguish one from the others. She also liked the new shopping center built across from our development with a grocery store, restaurants, and shops. Military life was also quite pleasant. My duties included organizing a post golf team and skeet-shooting range. Required duty was to attend officers' call Saturday mornings. I was instructed to inspect the Wilshire tank farm at least once a week since it was the repository of the fuel being shipped to Korea. My sole input to the Korean War was to suggest at one of the meetings—after watching a movie of our oil being removed from the boats by crane—that we push the barrels into the water and pick them up on shore. Believe it or not, the Army did just that so that turnaround time was cut substantially.

I was to become the Army's representative at the vocational school, which taught employees how to operate oil depots. My training was not going to waste. Through the school I met Bill Reed, the president of Time Oil Company. He later was the CEO of Chevron. It was from him that I learned that Wilshire Oil was the property of Lehman Bros., and Time Oil—nothing more than a small shack near the docks—was the principal company through which the oil was funneled. This raised my suspicions that something was not kosher here in the land where I was liable for the accuracy of the amounts shipped. My request to Archie Meyers, our civilian office manager who had a large locked filing cabinet, to read the procurement contract for the petroleum was denied. The background of Meyers was that he was a toll taker on the Golden Gate Bridge in San Francisco who had been sent several hundred miles south to this job. I was further bothered to read in the Los Angeles newspaper that Forrestal, Secretary of the Navy and the government officer in charge of hundreds of millions of barrels of oil supplies for the armed services, had either been pushed off or jumped from an upper-story window and was dead. It was ruled a suicide. I had to read the contract.

In the Brooklyn office near the dock where we had arrived I was introduced to five lieutenants, one of which I knew. Bobby Land, the national collegiate wrestling champion was there. I couldn't figure out why I was there. It occurred to me that Colonel Howard had asked me some weeks earlier on the telephone if I would like to take a petroleum course. I answered negatively since I had no interest in running an Army gas station or transport depot. I had performed decent services in procurement and hoped that I would be allowed to stay there but realized that I would have to have company duties as a captain which I had not yet become. My experience as a short term company commander and training officer showed no difficulties in performance. Where would petroleum training lead me?

We were all given instructions to report to a training school which turned out to be a storage warehouse. We were required to report for classes there in civilian clothes. We were told that we would be there for at least three months. I could not figure out why we were being trained there. There were plenty of schools equipped to provide technical training in New York City. I was puzzled at the fact that we were all paratroopers. No infantry men were present. I guessed that the Army didn't know what to do with us, like they had sent us to Germany to act as military police and do an unlikely job of training prisoners. The furniture in the building was crude and looked nothing like a school would. The plans of an unnamed gasoline depot were on our desks. The teacher talked about the refining process, the way to analyze octane grades, and other items that none of us knew before and had no desire to learn now. The paper that the maps and brochures used had what appeared to be Chinese letters in the margins. I speculated that they were printed somewhere in Chinatown to save money. I felt that the building facilities both from a physical and location sense was money saving way to have us learn a subject that we did not care to know. But we were in New York and enjoying it while our Army in Korea was losing men at an alarming rate. We weren't too worried about the outcome. After all, General Douglas MacArthur was in charge of the Korean theater and acting to destroy all hostile forces quite successfully.

The Triangle Shoe Company had both warehouse facilities and an apartment in New York for its buyers. Realizing that the living allowance would only allow us the minimum of accommodations, I asked my father whether I could use the company apartment. He agreed. I had civilian clothes from my Israel trip and my car had been delivered. Transportation facilities to the warehouse were not difficult to find. I drove to a site which had a parking lot and took public transportation to my destination. Land dropped out of the classes. We were told that he was ill. With all the strange things happening, I could only wonder whether he had been reassigned.

After classes ended, each of us was assigned to an instructor of a major oil company for on the job training. I was sent to Standard Oil of New York whose offices were in the southernmost end of Manhattan. There was a bar across the street in which my instructor had two martinis every day for lunch. No food. Just drinks. I remembered my tank chewing-tobacco incident and never touched a drop of alcohol while I was assigned to him. I never saw him drunk. I marveled that he could preserve his balance. The weeks I was with him were valuable. He taught me how an oil depot was run. This included security, analysis of the oil products stored there, how to keep track of the various classes of oil going in and out, and how to handle recalcitrant employees so they do not get angry to the point where they'll blow the place up. Safety measures were exhibited in all of Standard Oil's depots that we visited. I was separated from him after several weeks of this training feeling ready to go into the Army's oil business.

Two persons of the six of us were sent to posts unknown to me. We remaining four were all given orders to proceed to the West Coast. Each of us was assigned to a different city there. We were ordered to wear our uniforms and stay in New York, awaiting further orders. I made arrangements to vacate our borrowed apartment and send my two dependents to Wilkes-Barre. We were surprised when coming from a meeting. We were informed that Macarthur had been fired from his post in Korea and was being replaced. We remained in New York for a few days and told to leave for our destinations the same day MacArthur had a ticker tape reception in New York. It was a remarkable return to the Waldorf-Astoria Hotel where he would reside for the rest of his life. We had difficulty seeing him coming down the street because the crowd and paper strips were so thick. By climbing on a seat in a bar, I had a pretty good view through the window. I left New York as soon as I could get through the traffic.

The years I was stationed in Los Angeles were highly interesting. The Korean fighting had come to a standstill. MacArthur had successfully reduced the capabilities of both North Korean and Chinese troops from taking over South Korea. I had been informed that promotions would be few and far between. I needed to have a job to support my wife and two children if I left the service. I found that I could not support them to what was a minimum standard of living on a captain's pay. I had entered Loyola of Los Angeles night Law School with General Hayden's permission soon after I joined his post. I had little difficulties with the studies but it left me with almost no free time. I had relatives in the area and learned from my mother that she had a friend there who she knew quite well. She had been an actress on the Vienna stage and had married a well-known playwright from Wilkes-Barre by the name of Louie Weitzenkorn. He had brought her to live with him in Wilkes-Barre where he was writing radio shows. His most well-known one was Five Star Final. Television was taking over the radio stations and Louie was without a job. He became so depressed that he committed suicide in his apartment by turning on the gas in his kitchen and sealing the openings from outside air.

Zelda and I had brought Ursula, our nurse for Jimmy from Germany, to live with us. That enabled us to go to his house which looked like a mansion to us, and met a number of people there among whom were his sister Thelma who had just finished making a movie with Ethel Barrymore called *The Corn is Green*. Charles could not have been more cordial. He started the conversation by saying that he had seen me on a television quiz show and that if I was to go on another one he knew a good makeup artist. I asked him whether he stayed up all night watching television. He said he watched quiz shows because sometimes talent came out of them. I said that I knew that I wasn't photogenic but that I had won a number of things on the show without the makeup, including a television set. They were quite expensive in those days. Did he need another quiz show winner?

I asked him about Ilse, and he introduced her to me. I had never met her. It was several years since I had been in Wilkes-Barre. He told me that she had been hired as a talent scout and showed a lot of promise. I told him that my wife had been to the acting school in Steamboat Springs, was a rival to Julie Harris (then in a Broadway show), and would like to star in a movie.

He asked whether she had ever been in one, and I told him that she had starred as an extra in *Die Sterne Lugen Nicht* made in Geiselgasteig near Munich. He asked Ilse how the show was received in Germany, and she answered that if Zelda had the lead instead of being an extra, it might have been released and not been stopped by the censors. The lead had a nude part. I don't remember whether I thought that was complimentary or not. I also had never been told by Zelda what kind of film it was. No wonder she never wanted me to see it.

This Sunday party led to a number of meetings with people employed in Los Angeles's largest industry. I felt that if I could pass the Bar there, I could get a job which might pay us more than the Army. Unfortunately, life is something that you cannot control. It sometimes controls you, as I soon discovered.

The Schnees were not the only people we met socially. One couple was the Schnaders. Zelda's roommate at the University of Chicago had married Bob Schnader who was a lawyer in State politics. He was a political enemy of the Congressman from Whittier named Richard Nixon and always referred to him as "Tricky Dicky." This was because Nixon had aides break into his competitor's (Helen Gahagen Douglas) election office and remove documents from there which helped him win that election. I suspect that it was a practice move for Watergate years later. Bernie Janis had left the Army years earlier. He had managed to get married in a civil ceremony in Munich and get a special act passed in Congress to allow his wife Gerda to come into the United States in spite of the Walter-McCarren Act. He worked in the Broadway Department Store while Gerda sold Jiffy-Joint curtain rods to department stores and hardware stores. I had three uncles and their families living there. My office secretary, called in to report being late that day since her teenage brother died of a drug overdose he had taken in Tijuana, his favorite visiting place.

We certainly were able to fit into the community. We did not try because of the rampant drug trade. We felt that it was the wrong place to bring up children, especially since I would not be making enough money to live in a better neighborhood for years, if ever. The only job I felt certain I could get was to sell shoes in a Triangle Shoe Store. I was also disturbed about the Top Secret papers I was required to sign since I felt that they were part of a cover-up of the secret Army Macarthur had built with huge funds raised from cooperative suppliers such as Lehman Brothers and Forrestal. I figured that if they could proceed with this destruction of our legal chain of command, I wanted no part of it.

Ilse had no way to support herself since her English although excellent was strongly accented. My mother had kept in social contact with the Schnees in Bridgeport, Connecticut, who controlled MGM Studios in Hollywood. She called them and was told that Charles and Thelma, two of their children, were in Los Angeles, and were working at the studio. She mentioned that Ilse needed a job. They told her to send her to them and they would, in the meantime, check her credentials. Computers were not so efficient in those days. My mother gave the Schnees my telephone number, and Zelda gave me the information that Charles Schnee had called me and asked me to visit him at his home in Beverly Hills this coming Sunday. I cancelled a golf game I had with my Uncle Charlie and asked him if he knew Charles Schnee. He told me that he was MGM's chairman of the board and probably the number one producer in Hollywood. He had never met him but heard that he was a tough guy to deal with.

CHAPTER 5

Triangle Shoe Company

Neptune Moving Company had an arrangement with IBM to move its equipment around the country. The Kirschenbaums of Purchase, New York, owners and friends of my parents, moved what items we had accumulated in various residences in Europe and California. We left our home in Lakewood on October 18, 1953, and I started working in a Triangle Shoe Store in Wilkes-Barre, Pennsylvania, on October 21. Our car had three adults, two children, and one dog in a small seating area for the three days of driving. We moved into my mother-in-laws home where we stayed for about two months. I received my orders to report to Indiantown Gap that weekend. I was visited by the commanding officer of the 109th Field Artillery Unit who said that he needed an S-3 (military training officer) and I had a record of doing that. I thanked him for the opportunity but said that there was no way I could stay away from my job for weekends regardless of the possible increase in grade to Major since I had no income to feed my family and no desire to consider further service in the Army. I had transferred into the Reserve and was eligible to resign from it waiving all benefits from it.

The first few weeks of my job as a clerk in the store were educational. I was lucky that the manager took the time to show me the details of running a retail operation selling footwear and related items. We had X-Ray machines which showed the feet of customers in the selected shoes. We had dye kits to match the colors of cloth shoes specified by female customers. We also sold handbags, hosiery, and umbrellas plus other incidentals. We had few problems with inventory since a great deal of the merchandise was distributed from the warehouse on the floors both below and above the selling floor. The store was in a secondary location so that another Triangle Shoe in a prime location nearby attracted many more customers. Nevertheless, I was paid on a percentage basis of sales which amounted to more money than I was getting as a Captain. I had a lucky break when our manager was injured in an accident and had to stay out of the store for some time. The regular employees worked with me overtime to fill in the paper work at the end of the day and the inventory requests. I was busy seven days a week during that period.

A Colonel came into the store during a very busy period and requested that we go into the rear office for a conversation. He introduced himself as being from the Inspector General's Department. He wanted to know what I knew about the Forrestal Case and why I had quit the Army. I told him that I knew nothing about Forrestal except that there was a possible motive in his suicide or murder. I told him that I had been a procurement officer in Germany and had learned a great deal about the requirements of military contracts. Since they were on forms amounting to German reparations they were not standard contracts. However, I was trained to run an oil depot, which I had neither requested or desired, learned how to jump out of planes and land safely, and was never required to jump after the course completion causing a reduction in pay, was put in charge of oil shipments to Korea from the Time Oil Company which was a subsidiary of the Wilshire Oil Company ostensibly controlled by Lehman Brothers, one of whom was a U.S. Senator. It caused me to think that there might be an irregularity in procurement. I was not allowed to see the contract. A civilian employee in the office I had in San Pedro had been transferred there from San Francisco with specific instructions not to let anyone see it. I had been able to get it out of our filing cabinet, and the copies did not show a price. A bidders list was not attached. I had no idea as to whether there was any illegality involved, but I did not want to be associated with anything which could turn out to be another "Tea Pot Dome" scandal. I thought that there might be a connection between Forrestal and Lehman to provide the money for MacArthur's mission to move Chiang's troops out of Taiwan and into China. The privately bought LSI's had to be paid for, somehow. When MacArthur was fired, the mission collapsed. That could have opened up a giant can of worms. If Forrestal was involved, he would have been in disgrace. That was my idea of a possible motive for a national hero, which he certainly was.

The Colonel left. For refusing to show up for military drills, I was discharged from the service with full honors about a year later. Having been a West Point graduate, the Army felt to me as if it were a fraternity. It was really. I felt pain in leaving this club. I felt that I had no choice. Time heals all wounds. As much as I disliked West Point, I loved Army life.

I decided that I needed to increase my store's place in the firm from near last to first. There was a drugstore called Whalen's near Public Square at which many of the nearby merchants would take a coffee break at 10:00 a.m. every morning. I attended this informal meeting because I could meet my fellow merchants there. Claire Rosenberg, who ran a nurses' uniform shop around the corner from my store, was a very successful merchant. In spite of being off of South Main Street, she always had customers in her store. I bought her enough cups of coffee to find out why. She would visit nurses' training schools in our geographic area and, at each of their gatherings before graduation, would put on a display of uniforms, sometimes with models and sometimes not. I asked her whether she sold the shoes to go with the uniforms. She did not. I asked her if I could go along with her to present our nurse's oxfords. She said, "Why not?"

At my first showing at the Mercy Hospital's nursing class, I was prepared with two pairs of nurses' oxfords to show a few students, I thought. What a shock it was to be on stage after some ceremonies facing a graduating class of several hundred students. Claire introduced me, and I recited my unprepared lecture. We were carrying three brands of nurses' oxfords: Red Cross, Natural Bridge, and our own. I told them that if they came into my store and bought a pair, I could receive permission to give them a 15 percent discount. And if they brought any family members with them, I would extend the same privilege to them. They would have to register with me after the meeting for this privilege. I had more than a hundred signatures before I left the room. Because of my store's location in the same building which was used to distribute our merchandise, there were plenty of inventories on hand. I alerted my other clerks that we should expect a big day tomorrow. The "big day" turned out to be a perfectly normal one. It gave me time to alert our firm's buyers about the discount. They were quite unhappy about it, saying that our markup was not high enough to allow this as a regular item, but they would allow it one time. I woke up the next morning with a bad cold—probably from contact with the crowd of students I had registered the day before. I received a call about noon from one of the clerks that I had better get down there since they were swarming with customers. I put a painter's mask on and walked into a crowd of both nurse customers and their families. This continued for weeks. Our inventory buyers were so pleasantly surprised that they took my wife and myself out to dinner the next weekend night and used the same program in other towns where there were nursing schools. The system worked well enough that I got the title of assistant manager with a higher pay base.

Our injured manager returned to a very profitable store. I was moved to one of our five Scranton stores on the corner of Penn and Lackawanna Avenues. The manager had retired. This meant a commute of fifteen miles with no car. I borrowed one of the car returns—district managers turned their company cars in after one hundred thousand miles, and they were sold to used-car dealers in the area—and I never had any way to get one. I was promised a new one if I raised the store's volume to an increase of more than $100,000 annually. That was a lot of money for a popular priced shoe store with competition from four other company stores, although with different names and shoe brands.

There was a dress shop next door to mine. I used to read the trade publications. The *Boot and Shoe Reporter* was my favorite, among several others. I learned that there was a shoe chain in Seattle which had put in dresses so that they could offer a combination price which would benefit the overall sales. Its name was Nordstrom's. I received permission to try it in Scranton. It worked a little but not enough to excite any of the management. We would have had to set up a totally different buying office at considerable expense. The firm had access to all the capital needed but decided to put it elsewhere into additional stores in chain expansion.

We did have some interesting businesses in Scranton, which

was very good for us. Our Tom Brown store (outlet operation)—
with shoes that did not sell regularly quickly enough displayed
on tables and racks—did very well. So did our Enna Jettic store
along with the Park Lane one. My store held its volume nicely,
but I could not get the growth that I'd had in Wilkes-Barre. I
would sometimes go after closing across Penn Avenue to Kelly's
Irish Bar to meet other merchants who congregated there. I
met among many others Bill Kane, the district manager of the
A&P grocery stores. He had a marvelous grasp of Irish wit and
had a wonderful personality. Eventually, he became president of
A&P and conveyed sales messages which were never considered
anything but good advice. I asked him how I could build up
my store's volume. He said that you have to give the customers
something that nobody else has. In my case, with four other stores
and no special buyers for dresses with shoes, give them additional
time to shop. The merchants agreed to close at 5:00 p.m. Make
it 6:00 p.m. Open at 8:00 a.m. with one-hour specials. I tried,
and it worked beautifully.

Our warehouses, scattered and small, were to be consolidated
into one larger warehouse in the Edwardsville section of Wyoming
Valley. Since I had built a house near there pretty much copying
the one we had in California, I was asked to try to secure land
which belonged to the Glen Alden Coal Company. It was a small
several acre piece adjacent next to the busiest drive-in restaurant
in Wyoming Valley called Kearney's.

Charles Kearney had studied law and worked during summers
selling hamburgers across the road which was U.S. 11. He was
able to buy his piece of rented land from Glen Alden Coal
Company which had excavated about fifteen acres along the
highway creating a swamp because a stream ran into it with no
single outlet into the nearby Susquehanna River. Charles had
gradually filled about one acre alongside the highway. He paved

the lot and put up posts with phones into the shack with numbers on the posts. He hired girls of college age as waitresses and had them dress in skimpy summer dresses. He literally stole all of Barney's business, his competitor, with the combination of sexual appeal and location since the largest population was able to turn right into his property. U.S. 11 was the main highway between Kingston and Harrisburg and had a traffic count of more than twenty-five thousand cars per day. Charles built a permanent building to replace the shack and married one of his waitresses. He made enough money so that he never went back to college. I was one of his frequent customers when going to Wyoming Seminary, my Prep School. It was walking distance away.

My working days in Scranton sometimes ended with a visit to a bar on Penn Avenue. It catered to businessmen, many of whom worked for the A&P regional headquarters up the street. I met Bill Kane there. He was the district manager for northeastern Pennsylvania. His repertoire of Irish jokes was marvelous. He told me that he was looking for a location along U.S. 11 and near the new Acme Store, which apparently was doing the best grocery business in Wyoming Valley. I was familiar with the location since it was across from Kearney's. When I told him that, he suggested that I meet with Walter Robbins who had built a number of his stores. I managed to do so. Walter told me that he had A&P in many locations and was not interested in any more since he already had a risk in so many. He also said that if I was able to buy the land across from the Acme and spend millions of dollars to drain it and fill it, it might turn out to be a good location.

I made it a point to attend the next Saturday Triangle meeting in Wilkes-Barre. I hadn't been invited, but I knew that the firm was not happy with its downtown offices. The number of vehicles it was using was rising, and the location itself was not convenient for my father who walked there from his Kingston residence whenever he was in town. The Glen Alden location was just over a mile away from it. He told me that the site would be a good one for Triangle and to see the Glen Alden manager about buying it. I did. He was a retired Colonel and we were quite compatible with each other, even though he certainly outranked me. He agreed to sell us the front few acres adjacent to Kearney's and a gas station on the corner. He pointed out that a shoe warehouse would be okay, but we could not put a grocery store on it since he had made a deal with Acme that he would not allow a competitor on the land. Triangle decided to buy it in any event.

In a subsequent conversation with Bill Kane, I mentioned that we had purchased the land that he wanted but were going to use it ourselves. He said that he would put a store on the swampland behind the property if the restriction on the front property did not apply to the back. I asked him to have his firm's attorney check it out. He did and told me to buy the swampland. I was about to go into the shopping center business. First, I had to get Triangle to swap the front few acres for a larger acreage in the rear of the swampland. Sandy Weiss agreed with me that we needed more land for the Triangle than the smaller front parcel, and he took the job of constructing the new warehouse on it. He did a good job. All executives had their own offices. I did not get one since I was not an executive. I was allowed a desk in the main conference room as a place to receive mail when the project was finished. I was expected to be on the road as both a district manager and site selector. It was a perfect job for me.

The job of filling the swamp and financing the purchase of the swampland was not difficult. I was steered to the officer of a branch of a Scranton bank in Wilkes-Barre who took me into the president's office and vouched for me to the extent that I was able to walk out with a million-dollar check. I was personally liable, of course, but at that time I had no appreciable assets. On showing it to my father, he said that I should take the family into the deal. He thought there might be substantial jealousy because of the profits that should emerge from a shopping center to be built on the property. Since I would need more money to complete it, Triangle (with its triple-A rating) could make the financing possible at a lower rate than I could obtain. I agreed.

Glen Alden was a New York Stock Exchange company which had hardly ever sold land in the area because of the danger of mine settlement—plus the fact that there was so much land available, they could not get a decent price for it. This land required fills but not much since it was almost at road level. They owned sixteen acres adjacent to it of swampland usually filled with water and the home of the biggest rats I ever saw. Acme stores had leased land across Route 11 and was the first store of a line of stores which had space between it and the Sears Roebuck Store about three hundred feet south of it. When Acme moved in, Glen Alden Coal gave them assurance that they would not allow another competing chain on their frontal strip across the highway.

In my conversation with Bill Kane at the bar, I told him what was going on in Edwardsville. He said that they were interested in the location and would do business with me to put up one of their stores across the road on the level piece which I had already under contract. That was not possible because of the restriction in the deed I had bargained for, which precluded their store. Bill was sure after conference with his company's lawyer that the sixteen-acre hole in the ground was not affected by the Acme agreement. Because of its size and the tremendous cost to fill it, the retired Colonel who represented Glen Alden agreed to sell it to me personally for $100,000. He would prepare a lease, which would allow the bank they dealt with to lend me the money.

This was 1956. I had received permission from the Chief Judge of the Pennsylvania Supreme Court to take the Pennsylvania Bar Exam, provided that I would serve a clerkship in Rosenn, Jenkins, and Greenwald's office with Harold Rosenn as my proctor. This was subject to Bar Association approval. Loyola confirmed my grades as being satisfactory. The Bar Association approved it after a heated meeting. No one had passed the Bar in this manner since 1926, although many had tried. I worked out a schedule so that I could oversee the Scranton store in the daytime and work in the law office in Wilkes-Barre at night and Sundays for four years. I believe that it was more trying for my wife than me. She had the three children to worry about and a decorating business she started to help pay the bills. It wasn't pleasant doing this, but I figured that I had no choice. I intended to own my own business, and this was one way to do it.

The bank approved the loan. I had no money to apply to the required landfill. I knew that Connolly Construction was tearing down a hill in Luzerne, a neighboring community, and was paying to deposit it in a landfill. My information came from the locker room in the YMCA where I occasionally used the pool and played squash at noon when I was in town. I proposed that they deposit the removed clay on my land and leave a driver and leveling machine to spread it. It needed a large six-foot culvert to channel the storm water flow causing the water in the fill to make it a swamp. The culvert worked beautifully to dry up the land. Ed Fewins had a contract down the road a few miles to remove the culm from a coal breaker and saved travel expenses by depositing it in our hole. Connolly's grading machine plus a compression machine combined the clay and culm to where we had a solid base. The culvert was paid for by advance rents I was getting from new tenants who wanted to be in the shopping center I was creating. My father had a long experience in the building business and he insisted that I sell shares in the Narrows Shopping Center to spread the risk of failure. He was an investor in downtown real estate where he had made his fortune and was afraid that the shopping center might suffer the same fate as the downtown stores. I always did what he wanted and sold shares to my cousins retaining the right to manage the center with a 6 percent commission. I did not know then that he owned only one third of the Triangle Shoe Company stock and was concerned that the cousins would be jealous of the potentially very profitable real estate venture in their backyards. I never felt that way but agreed with Sandy Weiss that shopping centers were the wave of the future. My sister Nancy Klein who lives in Scarsdale told me about a neighbor living near her who was building an enclosed Mall in nearby Connecticut. I was always on the lookout for more stores and met with him. We both agreed that the shopping center revolution had no education facilities and needed one.

He agreed to take a look at what I was doing and made some excellent suggestions. We felt that although there were enough real estate organizations already, a shopping center organization should be founded. He named it the International Council of Shopping Centers. I became one of its charter members. The Connecticut Life Insurance Company had already financed several shopping centers. To protect their investments, they hired a portion of the Connecticut University's buildings during the summer of 1957 at Storrs near Hartford and ran classes there using top real estate officials. We had nearly a hundred developers in attendance. We decided that we would not register as a trade organization until we had a hundred dues-paying members. That number was achieved New Year's Eve at the Starlight Roof of the Waldorf Astoria. It turned out to be a very valuable source for me in buying and selling commercial property later. The

ICSC has about thirty-five thousand members today and is truly international.

All this activity took place during construction of the Narrows Shopping Center. I bought an old bus, stripped the seats out of it and used it as an office while the Shopping Center was going up. The Triangle offices and warehouse building was being erected at the same time under Sandy Weiss's direction. I had nothing to do with it. I wish I had at that time since no office was reserved for me. When I moved into the building, I was assigned to a desk in the conference room where my father could watch what I was doing when I was there—which was not often. I was on the road and in Rosenn's office.

At the end of the four-year period in Rosenn's office Harold suggested to me that I go to Philadelphia to take Leonard Levin's course on Pennsylvania Procedure. He felt that even though I had spent countless hours in the County Courthouse I still required the procedural knowledge which usually shows up on the examinations. I was in a rooming house on the campus of the University of Pennsylvania. The courses Levin presented were for the most part what I already knew. The Rosenn attorneys were extremely helpful when I needed a question answered. When searching titles I used Marty Haslinsky in the Registrar's office to look for the possible errors. When preparing a Devil's Advocate case for Henry Greenwald, I used the County Law Library, which was open twenty-four hours a day and weekends. No college courses could have been more thorough.

The Bar examinations were held at Temple University on two consecutive days. We were allowed to bring typewriters in. I had a Swiss portable which I dropped on the steps going into the classroom where the exam was given. We were allowed to write our answers in longhand which for me was no advantage. My handwriting while legible is not good. The questions were not too tough to my surprise, but I felt that I needed an exam judge who had a lot of patience with my lengthy answers. I must have had one since I passed and surprised everyone in the office including me.

When I returned to the Triangle Shoe conference room there was a lady waiting to see me. She said that she had called Rosenn's office, and they referred her to me. It was a family matter which involved her daughter who was pregnant by an Edwardsville soldier who was serving overseas. I knew the soldier's father who was a Councilman on the Edwardsville Council. He knew his son's address, so I got in touch with him. We received what was to me a substantial sum over what I thought Orphan's court would have granted. My fee to the mother was ten dollars. On the child's twenty-first birthday, the mother brought her into my office and introduced her. She was an attractive lady, and I thought that the mother did not pay too much for what she received. That was all the family law I ever had. My specialty was Real Estate Law. I drew up a sample shopping center lease for landlords. The ICSC published it as a sample to be used in Pennsylvania. I was invited to speak to New York lawyers at a CLE Conference in the Plaza Hotel. They knew more about the business than I did, but the lease is still used. It came in quite handy when public disturbances occurred. The Triangle Shoe Company had operating stores in Brooklyn when riots occurred, putting the store out of business at Fulton and Nostrand Streets. It had another one adjacent to the field in Kent, Ohio, when the National Guard Troops shot civilians, causing that store to close. The lease protected the company in both cases. They are standard clauses in commercial leases these days. They were not then.

The most important thing I had learned in Rosenn's office is that you must protect your client at all legal costs. You must keep them out of court. Cases won not infrequently cost the client more than it cost him to get the judgment. Joseph Savitz was a mortgage specialist. When my business became larger, he was the voice of caution and saved me during times when the business of the moment went sour. There were a few of those incidents. However, I followed my father's advice to be lucky rather than smart, and I was.

I had made in some years more money than I ever had at the Triangle Shoe Company. Bob Gintel did very well for me as a stockbroker, and I used some of his suggestions to add to my cash positions. As my net worth grew, I decided that I could leave the Triangle and set up my own real estate company. There was enough income to send my kids to top colleges and help them to get started in their own successful businesses or professions. Zelda was also doing well as an interior decorator.

It was time to move to my native state of Florida. I gave notice that I would leave at the end of 1971. This was changed to July 1 of 1972, when my mobile home park (then under construction) would have one hundred tenants, and Sandy Weiss would take the real estate duties over—which he did, in the fall.

Bob Gintel invited a group of his friends to come to some of his vacation sites which were in Barbados and northern Canada. Zelda and I were privileged to be at some of them. Zelda liked the Caribbean ones, but did not go on the fishing trip to Great Bear Lake in northern Canada. That was one of my most interesting trips and will be better explained a little later. Bob's wife Barbara loved to entertain and gave a birthday party for Bob at which he arrived in a make-up condition whereby he could not be recognized even by his wife. He had a great sense of humor. Because he met people easily, he was able to get company information which aided greatly in stock selection. Bob Gintel invited me to join his group which was going fishing on Great

Bear Lake. I accepted and spent a lovely week fishing and visiting the town of Coppermine on the edge of Baffin Bay.

On our trip back from Great Bear Lake, we stopped at Yellowknife. Bob Gintel had developed a serious infection from a skin penetration by a fish hook. There were no medical services at the Lodge, and the accident had to be addressed as soon as we returned to civilization. While he was being treated, I wandered around town and went into a bar which appeared to have quite a few patrons. I saw a lone Indian sitting at a table and decided that I could get some information from him if I was lucky. I was. He wanted to talk, and I filled the bill. I asked him his name and received his response that I must be new to those parts since people never gave their names to strangers. He offered me a first name, which I felt was not his real one. He would not tell me what tribe he was from, but mentioned that if I was trying to avoid the Mounties, Yellowknife was the best place to be. Workers were always needed so that your background, whether criminal or not, was immaterial. The mine was not difficult to work in summer or winter—the temperature was the same year round underground. The pay was more than he could spend. Not surprising since the business district contained few stores. The bars were the only social outlets available, except for the churches which, he stated, were poorly attended. There were legalized brothels. I had noticed the apparent shortage of women on the streets. When I got up to leave, he pulled out a hunting knife, put it on the table, and told me to stay there until he was ready to leave. Fortune was always in my favor since Bob Gintel came into the bar looking for me and said that he had made arrangements for us to visit the gold mine as soon as possible. The Indian looked away, and I left in a hurry.

The mine was fascinating. I had visited a coal mine and found this one to be quite different. The ore was removed similarly but treated with large chemical baths. A large volume of arsenic was captured and very little gold. Outside the mine shaft, there were small mountains of arsenic. The gold was sequestered and out of site. My thoughts of gold nuggets coming out like coal were changed. There were no nuggets here. Just earth containing specks of gold that had to be removed by a chemical process.

Bob Gintel was the best securities salesperson I ever ran into. He investigated personally all firms in which he and his clients bought stock. He did have an unusual sense of humor! Going through US Customs in Toronto, he told the inspector that the box in which I had some fish I was bringing home contained drugs. I passed a rigid inspection. Jokes of this nature were an anathema to me, but I never took them seriously. Bob had included me into his social circle of friends, and I was delighted to meet a portion of the world that I would never come into contact with otherwise. He was also a very good stock advisor and one of the reasons I could afford to put my children through college.

Bob turned out to be an excellent long-term stock advisor. He had turned my sister's original $25,000 stock purchase into $3,000,000 over many years. I withdrew mine when they reached over $1,000,000 and used them for down payments on many real estate opportunities. Sol Horwitz was a classmate of mine who had married the daughter of a principal owner of Consolidated Cigar Company. A 110,000-foot building, originally the distribution and office center of Kirby five and ten cents stores, had been closed and put on the market for sale. I purchased it for my wife for $400,000, basically because I knew that Sol had put the building into excellent shape for his company, which vacated it. I rented it to Harte Hanks Publishing, which needed more space. They later expanded to another location, twice as big, and I sold it for a $400,000 profit. When I called Sol to thank him for the excellent job be had done, I was surprised to learn that he had died in an airplane accident going to a convention in New Orleans for mayors of smaller cities. He was the mayor of Scarsdale, New York. Some of our guys had gone into politics. Some had received generals stars. I had my own business.

Ed Tutin was an employee of the Gintel operation. I had occupied a fishing boat with him on the trip and had traveled with him by air to Coppermine. Ed had some disagreements with Bob and they separated and no longer worked together. I lost contact with him and wondered whether a similar practical joke was involved. I never had the answer to this.

Why be a soldier when with less effort you can be a millionaire? All of us in the professional military are aware of the failures and betrayals that can bring us down from being promoted to general to forced retirement early with a very modest income and no training to enter a different profession. Eisenhower used to advise that we should be wary of the military-industrial trap the country had run into. We had The Teapot Dome scandal after our Civil War which was not a one-time aberration but was followed by others throughout the course of our history. I began to realize the dangers to our military system when assigned to military procurement.

Zelda Klein and I knew each other our entire lives. Her mother, Anna Newman, was a schoolmate of my mother, and they remained close both in their school and married years. Zelda's brother Howard and I were only ten weeks apart in age. We saw a great deal of each other growing up and, summers, went to Camp Brunonia in Casco, Maine. We played on basketball teams in Wyoming Seminary school days. Howard was a better athlete than me, but not as good a student academically. He entered the Navy in 1944, and was discovered to have Addison's disease at his New York State Fingerlake Station. He was there the entire war.

He went from the Navy directly into his father's and uncle's Klein Auto Parts business. He did not attend college. He married Syvia Hoder in his twenties. She was from Scranton. They had three children. He died early in life from stomach cancer, probably induced by the steroids required to keep his Addison's disease under control. His sister Zelda, who became my wife, outlived him by many years. She passed away after an operation to reduce the size of her aortic artery. She was seventy-eight.

I was away from home most of the time. Zelda was also away to a lesser extent since she became a successful interior designer. Her business required her to be in New York much of the time. We had separate paths in our businesses. Our marriage lasted fifty-seven years until her death on April 29, 2005. While we were married, we were a relatively content couple. We knew each other as friends during our lives. We had our differences, but they were always settled. Our relationship developed more deeply as we reached our seventies. Her loss to me was greater than I ever imagined it would be. Before my grandson's finding me a replacement on Match.com, I had lost the will to live. Lois Lane straightened me out. A little over two years later, we were married in Florida. My three children were present at the wedding. I was starting my new life, which was totally different from the old one.

My life was full of interesting details mostly consisting of friendships made and lost, business speculations successful and otherwise. My airplane business was certainly a departure from the norm. It had its exciting moments. Some speculative activities did not work out well. Most did. The twists and turns of anyone's life define not only character but the pleasantness of living. Thank heaven for the pleasures which make the problems bearable. I decided to stop trying to become wealthier. My life took a definite change in direction. My principal residence had shifted to Florida for many years. My living accommodations changed from small apartments to a larger permanent home which we now occupy. Having been born in Florida, I decided to end it there.

Most of my friends and family members from childhood, college and business have passed away. The few who are still living are scattered over our country. Twenty-seven classmates turned up at our sixty-fifth West Point reunion. I doubt that many will be at the seventieth. I hope to be there.

My life had so many interesting twists and turns that I feel it was truly worth putting it into published words. I had pursued knowledge and contacts with people who made changes in our lives. I realized my life's ambition, which was to raise exceptional children. That was what my father said John Rockefeller advised him to do when they were working on real estate accumulations for Rockefeller's real estate companies. In that I have succeeded. My son Jimmy, now deceased, was an exceptionally good antitrust attorney known worldwide in his profession and represented many of the world's largest companies. Susan Weiss-Shoval, with her gifted mind, achieved the highest grades recorded at the College of Insurance, and married an exceptional Israeli lawyer who directed their business to where a major international insurance company, Clal, paid them a king's ransom for the business. The two of them still are at work trying to catch and pass our country's wealthiest people with their new company called Ambit. My son Jeffrey married Nancy Freeman, the girl in the next dormitory to his at MIT. She is now VA's Chief of Oncology at Brown University's Medical College. Jeffrey had patented products, mostly in the communications equipment field. He achieved the highest level of Boy Scouting as an Eagle

Scout. He developed a number of companies. He entered politics and ran for school board in Lincoln, Rhode Island. He was elected school director against the opposition of both political parties with 75 percent of the vote on a write-in basis. He was later made the board's chairman. He is still collecting stock in various technical companies if he believes that they have a strong chance of success. Try to beat that.

Saturday morning after a previous night's seasonal cocktail party at the Huntsville Golf Club. Up to twenty-five laps in our swimming pool. What a struggle since my left knee replacement. Fixing worn-out sections of my body was painful but necessary so that I could finish this memoir.

With the transfer of most of my assets after the sale of all my real estate except for a few Florida properties to the Legacy Group in Sarasota, my life changed substantially. My former wife had used the owner of an insurance group, Don Wallace, on the recommendation of Charles Githler of Investment Seminars Incorporated. Charles used Louis Rukeyser as one of his principal speakers, Zelda felt that her liquid assets were safest using his advice. Wallace turned out to be an excellent advisor. After Zelda's death, I felt that I should reopen the contact and turn all liquid assets, including her estate, over to him.

Wallace had grown in the intervening years from a personal advisor to a major insurance broker specializing in the sale of variable annuities from Lincoln Life Insurance Company. I had some knowledge of this type of investment since I had obtained a federal license to sell this type of security from the Travelers group. The economy in 2005 was at a boiling point, and I knew that it was like a bubble ready to burst. One of the real estate salesmen I had been working with in Coldwell Banker's Naples office had held a position as treasurer in a major New York Stock Exchange Company. He had taken large short positions in several companies whose stock he felt was highly inflated in price. I was not successful in making any profits in the small short positions. I tried as a learning trial.

Realizing that what success I had investing in the stock market was due to superior knowledge gained from my business affairs and clubs such as Rotary, and charitable institutions in which I was actively engaged, I decided that now that I was no longer privy to such an advantage over the general public. It was time to change management of my affairs. Fortunately, I still have some Florida real estate, which although temporarily depressed, will allow me to regain some net worth. Life is never certain. This is a lesson that is hard to learn.

Now eighty-five, I have nine granddaughters, one grandson, and two great-grandchildren. This occurred without even trying. Two of my three children were healthy, well-educated, and satisfied with their mates. Jim had died of failure of his aortic artery five years after Zelda's untimely death in 2005. My new wife looked a little like Zelda, but had a different type of upbringing in the District of Columbia.

We were married in Temple Beth Shalom in Naples on May 10, 2007. The service was conducted by my niece, Rabbi Lisa (Weiss) Stern. The after-wedding dinner was held at our club at Pelican Bay. All my children and many of my friends attended, and as a social affair, it was quite successful. I detected an air of doubt among my children as to the long-term probability of success of this marriage, but Lois did her best to remove it and has been successful in her endeavor. We settled in a small coach house in the gated community of Kensington in Collier County. I was delighted with the location and the way she decorated it to make it feel like home.

Lois found the house she had been looking for most of her

life. Its master bedroom had twenty-foot ceilings, a balcony
for future use of expansion, and two separate bathrooms—one
for each of us. Mine has its own steam bath. The house was
an expanded display model of a 1987 builder and was under
complete renovation when she found it. The construction cost
to finish it to Lois' requirements was substantial. However, she
vowed that we would not move from it. The pool is quite scenic
and the yard at least as large as ours in Kingston, Pennsylvania.
It has a boathouse turned into a well-decorated office and gym.
It is set back from the highway by a wall and has two electrically
controlled gates. The house insulation has been expertly applied
so that no outside noise comes in. For finishing touches, the roof
has had shingles removed and replaced with the current hurricane
proof metal roof in vogue. All outside windows are hurricane
proof to 150-mph winds. We installed a gas driven generator to
keep electricity indoors in case of the loss of it for any reason. The
kitchen is a professional cook's dream with a gas stove, a cooking
appliance elevator, electric oven, and granite surfaces throughout.
Lois's brother decided to put cabinets in our dressing room closet
as a wedding gift. The seller was a Croatian apartment builder
who left us with an oar from a sunken 1862 British warship. It,
along with a life preserver, is over two hundred years old and
hangs on the wall of our roofed-in terrace by the pool.

Pictured above is the front of the beautiful new store in Winston-Salem, North Carolina. Herb Trageser, a veteran manager of the Massena store, is at the helm.

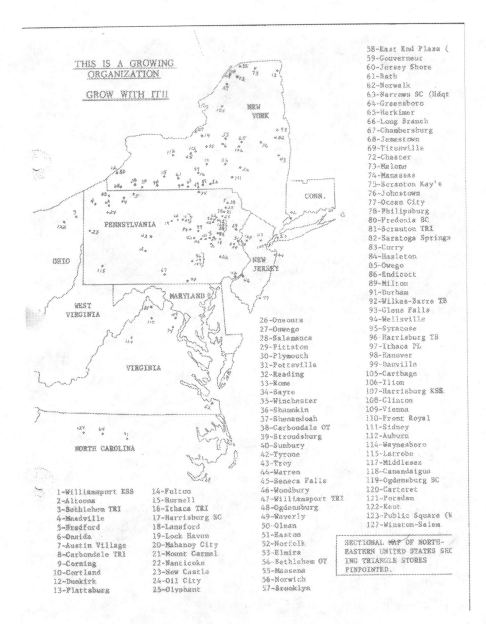

THIS IS A GROWING
ORGANIZATION

GROW WITH IT!!

NEW YORK

CONN.

PENNSYLVANIA

OHIO

NEW JERSEY

WEST VIRGINIA

MARYLAND

VIRGINIA

NORTH CAROLINA

38–East End Plaza (
59–Gouverneur
60–Jersey Shore
61–Bath
62–Norwalk
63–Barrows SC (Hdqt
64–Greensboro
65–Herkimer
66–Long Branch
67–Chambersburg
68–Jamestown
69–Titusville
72–Chester
73–Malone
74–Manassas
75–Scranton Kay's
76–Johnstown
77–Ocean City
78–Philipsburg
80–Fredonia SC
81–Scranton TRI
82–Saratoga Springs
83–Corry
84–Hazleton
85–Owego
86–Endicott
89–Milton
91–Durham
92–Wilkes-Barre TB
93–Glens Falls
94–Wellsville
95–Syracuse
96–Harrisburg TB
97–Ithaca PL
98–Hanover
99–Danville
105–Carthage
106–Ilion
107–Harrisburg KSS
108–Clinton
109–Vienna
110–Front Royal
111–Sidney
112–Auburn
114–Waynesboro
115–Latrobe
117–Middlesex
118–Canandaigua
119–Ogdensburg SC
120–Carteret
121–Potsdam
122–Kent
123–Public Square (W
127–Winston-Salem

26–Oneonta
27–Owego
28–Salamanca
29–Pittston
30–Plymouth
31–Pottsville
32–Reading
33–Rome
34–Sayre
35–Winchester
36–Shamokin
37–Shenandoah
38–Carbondale OT
39–Stroudsburg
40–Sunbury
42–Tyrone
43–Troy
44–Warren
45–Seneca Falls
46–Woodbury
47–Williamsport TRI
48–Ogdensburg
49–Waverly
50–Olean
51–Easton
52–Norfolk
53–Elmira
54–Bethlehem OT
55–Massena
56–Norwich
57–Brooklyn

1–Williamsport KSS
2–Altoona
3–Bethlehem TRI
4–Meadville
5–Bradford
6–Oneida
7–Austin Village
8–Carbondale TRI
9–Corning
10–Cortland
12–Dunkirk
13–Plattsburg

14–Fulton
15–Hornell
16–Ithaca TRI
17–Harrisburg SC
18–Lansford
19–Lock Haven
20–Mahanoy City
21–Mount Carmel
22–Nanticoke
23–New Castle
24–Oil City
25–Olyphant

SECTIONAL MAP OF NORTH-
EASTERN UNITED STATES SHO
ING TRIANGLE STORES
PINPOINTED.

Map of store locations does not show where the additional
20 stores were when I liquidated the chain.

BIRTH OF A SHOE CHAIN   By Aaron Weiss

THE PAST

Since this is an Anniversary Issue, it may not be amiss to answer the question which has been asked of me so many times and which may be of interest to some of you reading this bulletin. I have often been asked about the origin of this organization. "How did it come about?" Perhaps I wouldn't go into this, except for the fact that its origin was the result of one of the most unique and generous incidents I have ever experienced.

In 1921, I had been practicing law for about two years, and I had made no momentous inroads to a successful legal career. Having plenty of time on my hands, I visited one of my classmates in Bridgeport, Connecticut, who had made a considerable fortune in real estate. Bridgeport was booming. Real estate was very much in demand and these boys, Sam and Abe Schnee, were riding the crest of the wave. Sam, who was my classmate at law school, turned to me and said, "Aaron, why don't you go into the shoe business?" I replied that I didn't have any capital with which to start. I had known something about the shoe business because I worked in a shoe store during holidays and Saturdays to earn my tuition and expenses. "How much would it take?" Sam asked, and I replied, "It would probably take $15,000.00 to $20,000.00 to start on a substantial scale." Whereupon he took a checkbook out of his desk, and wrote out a check for $17,500.00. "Here it is, Aaron, and we are partners."

I was a little puzzled at first. We had no agreement, no understanding, and he had no security of any kind; I was to go ahead on the basis of our being "partners". With this money I came to the coal regions; but even then, I was advised that I had better look for a more fertile territory. Frankly, it was hard sledding at first. After about a year, my associates reminded me of the fact that they weren't really interested in the shoe business, but that they had given me this money merely to help me get started (which I knew). Whereupon I contacted my brothers, Morris and Ben, and asked them to take over their interest. Strange as it may seem, the Plymouth store pre-dated the Triangle, and it was the Plymouth store that was put into the pot as the principal investment on the part of Morris and Ben to cover their share in the business.

There was nothing sensational about the growth of the Triangle. Many businesses made much greater and faster progress. Frankly, I knew how to sell a pair of shoes, but I did not know the business. For a number of years, I was salesman, buyer, advertising manager, store sweeper and did all sorts of jobs which were not quite consistent with the so-called chain store "executive".

May I, at this time, pay my humble tribute to quite a number of the men and women in this organization who are with us today and who have contributed their talents and their brains to make a success of this organization. I am referring particularly to Leo Bergsmann, Harry Hickman, Sammy Harrison, Joe Silberman, Eva Nanstiel, Julia Blazes and last but not least, Oscar Alinikoff, Joe Pollack, "Fink" and Agnes McGeever. Many others have come and gone, but these people still represent the backbone of the organization.

I have not mentioned any members of the family -- for apparent reasons. Nor am I overlooking the valuable services rendered by others in the organization -- as the years went by -- particularly the managers and sales people, who are on the firing line and without whom the Triangle could not continue very long. I hope this business will continue to grow and prosper so that we may give greater remunerative recognition to those in the organization who are so clearly deserving.

THE PRESENT

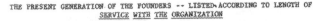

THE PRESENT GENERATION OF THE FOUNDERS -- LISTED ACCORDING TO LENGTH OF
SERVICE WITH THE ORGANIZATION

MORTON B. WEISS -- Born May 7, 1916, Coatesville, Pa. Education: Graduated
from Coatesville High School 1932, Harvard College 1936, Harvard Law School
1939. Member of the Bar of the Supreme Court of Pa. Occupation: Triangle
warehouse 1940, managed Pittston store 1941, District Manager 1942-1944.
Present position, Vice-President in charge of Merchandising and Secretary
of the Triangle Shoe Company. Offices held: Director, Nation Assoc. of
Shoe Chain Stores since 1950; Member of Board of Directors, United Fund of
Wyoming Valley since 1960; President, Jewish Community Center of Wyoming
Valley since 1959; Member of Board of Directors, Wyoming Valley Jewish
Committee. Member of: Kingston Rotary Club; Chester County Bar Assoc.;
Masonic Lodge, Number 355, Wilkes-Barre; Keystone Consistory, Scranton;
Irem Temple Shrine, B'nai B'rith Lodge and American Jewish Committee.

STANLEY M. WEISS -- Born September 25, 1918, Coatesville, Pa. Education:
Graduated from Coatesville High School 1936; University of Virginia 1936-
1939; graduated from University of Miami, Coral Gables, Florida 1940. Army
service (Engineers) 1942-1945. Overseas, European Theatre 1943-1945.
Triangle background: Began in Triangle Oneonta, New York, on floor. After
return from service, served as Manager of T.B. Pittston, #97 Wilkes-Barre,
Triangle Scranton, Park Lane Wilkes-Barre. Spent several years on road as
District Manager. At present, Vice-President in charge of Store Operations.
Married Miriam (Cissie) Cohen in January, 1941. Have two children--Cathey
Ann, a sophomore at Carnegie Tech in Pittsburgh, Pa.; a son, Stanley, Jr.,
a sophomore at Wyoming Seminary.

NORMAN J. SONDHEIM -- Born in Brookline, Massachusetts. Educated at
Brookline High School, Harvard College and Harvard Law School. Moved to
Kingston in 1940 and worked on the floor at the Triangle Store in Nanticoke,
Manager in Pittston until 1943. Military service 1943-1946. Present
position, Vice-President of Bags, Hosiery and Findings Department. Married
Evelyn Weiss in 1941. Three children: Alan, eighteen, a sophomore at
Brown; Majorie, fourteen, a freshman at Wyoming Seminary; and Mark eleven,
in sixth grade at Wyoming Seminary Day School.

STANFORD L. WEISS (Sandy) --- Born West Chester, Pa., January 28, 1927.
Moved to Kingston, Pa., 1941. Graduated Wyoming Seminary 1944, University
of Michigan 1949, Harvard Graduate School of Business Administration 1951.
U. S. Merchant Marine Cadet Corps 1944-1946. Assistant to Fashion Merchan-
dising Manager and Assistant Buyer, John Wanamaker, Philadelphia, 1951-1953.
1953-1961 with Triangle Shoe Company as salesman, Relief Manager, District
Manager, and now, Vice-President in Merchandise Department. Married in
January, 1949 to Geraldine London of Gary, Indiana. Two children: son,
Dick, born 1951 and daughter, Marilyn, born 1954. General Chairman,
Wyoming Valley United Jewish Appeal 1962; Trustee, Wyoming Valley Jewish
Community Center; Kingston Rotary Club.

NORMAN E. WEISS -- Born April 12, 1926, Daytona Beach, Florida. Attended
Wilkes-Barre and Kingston public schools. Graduated Wyoming Seminary in
1943, the United States Military Academy at West Point in 1946. Attended
the University of Loyola Law School in Los Angeles and admitted to practice
law in Luzerne County in 1960. Employed prior to joining the Triangle
Shoe Company in November of 1953 by the United States Army for 10½ years.
During this period, served 3½ years in Germany, the remainder of the time
in the United States. Trained to sell shoes under Heshie Harowitz, managed
the Triangle Store at 97 South Main Street, spent several years as District
Manager in Pa. and New York state, ran the Outlet Division for a brief period of time and is presently employed as Vice-President in the Real Estate
Division at Headquarters. Married Zelda Klein, three children, one dachshund.

2

"N.E.W." LEASES

ON

LIFE!

Norman E. Weiss

1961 has seen us off and running with new stores. In the month of March alone there was a relocation in Scranton, a new unit in Jersey Shore, in Greensboro, and in Winston-Salem. In the case of two of these stores, the leases were made two years prior to the opening. Such is the nature of the real estate business today that you must anticipate what an area's probabilities will be two years in advance, because most stores are being built for us today within shopping centers.

Our policy has been, and will continue to be, to close small, unprofitable units and shift the merchandise into larger and higher volume units. In other words, we must constantly run just to stay even, but to get ahead takes considerable doing. In this regard, I would like to point out that individual store operations make it easy or tough to lease new locations to a far greater degree than most people imagine.

For example, I had an odd experience a few months ago while meeting with a real estate developer to lease a storeroom in a new center that he was building in New Jersey. He told me that he had been in to one of our stores a few days previously, that the manager looked unkempt, the storeroom itself like a pigpen, and that he was not interested in leasing an operation to an organization with this type of housekeeping policy at any price. I was rather abashed; but when I went to the store to check on his remarks, I found that they were comletely justified. Needless to say, the situation has been cleared, but it cost us what could have been a profitable store.

On the other hand, I was recently with a Long Island developer who told me that his doughter goes to school in Troy and that he had asked to check the store in that town and buy several pairs of shoes. She reported back to him that the manager was charming, that she was fitted with several pairs of shoes, and that she liked the entire atmosphere of the storeroom, as well as being

purchased. This made negotiations with this particular developer extremely easy, and we were able to arrive at a more favorable lease than might otherwise have been the case. Hats off to Joe Morris.

You can see that running a storeroom has deeper ramifications than the register reading in many cases. Because of this, you affect the leasing of new stores in a far greater measure than you might think.

*   *   *   *   *

WE NEED

Your editors are conceited enough to believe that this current issue of "THE CHATTERBOX" has surpassed all of the past. We have instituted new techniques in preparation of the cover, and new methods of presenting various parts of the inside of this periodical to make it of greater interest to our readers. However, we plan a deluxe issue for the end of the year that we expect will dwarf this current beautiful issue. We cannot disclose at this time the motif of the December issue, but we do know it can only be as good as the material contributed. For that reason, we hope you will respond when we ask you for lots of interesting items about your stores.

*   *   *   *   *

CHAPTER 6

Flying

While with the Triangle Shoe Company and Later

Travel around the country was certainly educational for the real estate portfolio I expected to and did accumulate. The problem was that I spent too little time with my wife and children. I was determined to become wealthy, and real estate was the only way I could see to do it. The stock market was fairly good to me. That was because of Bob Gintel. He handled my account beautifully. I used my basement office to do my own trading and came out ahead. He did better. The market profits paid for my children's education. However, it did not add appreciably to my net worth. I had basic aviation training in the Army but never finished it since the war ended and half of the trainees were sent back to West Point. I was one of the first returned. In civilian life when I was making big enough income I could contemplate flying again. I could get home rapidly no matter where I was. Triangle Shoe was not paying me much of a salary, but it did reimburse much of my expenses, including the flying.

I bought an old Piper Tripacer as my first plane. My wife and kids loved the fact that all five of us could take trips to Williamsburg, Martha's Vineyard, and Florida. The plane was fabric covered. My father was astounded that it did not have a metal skin. He came up to the Forty Fort airport to examine it and asked the mechanic, Eddie Shuklis, if he thought it was safe. Eddie responded that he only fixed them. He wouldn't fly in them. My father decided that he would like to ride in it anyway. I no sooner got into the air with him than he said to take him down. To reach the required landing altitude I had to keep on climbing. He sharply disagreed. We landed safely. He never went into any of my planes again. That was a pity since I owned more planes which were far more sophisticated.

I never had instrument training in or out of flight school. Wyoming Valley has more than a fair share of instrument weather. On a return trip from Allentown in the Tripacer I went through clouds of snow which left me without any outside vision. With no instruments I was forced to fly with needle, ball, and airspeed. Al Bellsey, a former Navy pilot, had told me that if I got into instrument trouble call the Wyoming Valley tower and ask them to direct me into the Forty Fort airport which has a much lower altitude than the one in Avoca. The controller would allow me to land without instruments. I did this, broke out below the snow and found myself at a low elevation over the Susquehanna River. I traded this plane in for a Cessna well equipped 210.

There were quite a few pilots with private planes at Forty Fort. Luzerne County had an ad in our newspaper offering the airport for rent. Russ Smith was retiring from running the airport. In order to protect the airport from closing, seven of us who were pilots formed an organization and named it Anjil Aviation. The president, Gene Shlenger, was a Buick dealer from Scranton who had two daughters named Ann and Jill. I was elected the treasurer. We felt that we could not only run the airport well but also profitably. We made money in our repair shop, our gasoline sales, and training school. We lost money on our flights to Teterboro, Northeast Philadelphia, and Washington D.C. Since I was by that time rated commercially, instruments, and twin engine satisfactorily, I enjoyed the flights but not the fact that we were not making money. We sold the operation with our planes to a Pocono-based group operating their own airport next to the Pocono's only nudist camp. All our members of Anjil showed up—but no nudists! It was raining.

After I had several engine problems in single-engine planes, I decided to buy an Aerostar Piper 601P from 'Pug' Piper. He had it at Teterboro. It was a sales demonstrator which had every conceivable instrument which could fit on the plane at that time, including radar and ice removal equipment. It flew comfortably at twenty-five thousand feet since it was pressurized to that altitude. I kept the cabin pressure at eight thousand feet at all times during cross-country flights. Holding six people did not allow me to reach southern Florida without a fuel stop. At the Avoca airport was a factory where planes were equipped with additional gasoline tanks. I investigated and set up an appointment to have my plane modified. The modification never took place since the factory owner was convicted of smuggling drugs into Bill Scranton's private airport, and went to jail. Sidney Hinerfeld, a well-known Scranton realtor, tried to sell me the airport with its buildings. The price was right, but I decided that if I couldn't make money in the Forty Fort airport, I couldn't in Scranton either.

I listed about one thousand hours on my log. There were only a few close calls. One was in a Twin Comanche. I had refueled in Nassau and had an engine cut out on me on takeoff from the Fort Lauderdale airport where we had stopped to go through customs on our way back to Miami. I was not able to climb on the one partially functioning engine. I reached Opalocka and the live engine cut out on landing. We were safely towed into a repair hanger. The same plane had been caught in the jet stream of a commercial jet taking off in the Newark airport, causing one wing to drop. Full throttle and luck kicking the rudder away from the turn gave me enough altitude to keep me in the air. My solution was to sell the plane and buy another one.

I bought a turbo prop Beechcraft from a pilot trying to sell it in the Cincinnati airport which we needed in our air taxi service. I remember that it had a bathroom in the cabin. It wasn't fast, but customers on the flights to Teterboro liked it. It was one of the few planes which ran profitably. Ted Smith, who was the designer of the Aerostar, designed this plane as well. President Eisenhower used it when moving about the country since it was then the only twin certified to take off on one engine, which was a unique safety feature.

When we started Anjil in operation, we had income streams figured out. One source was to have airmail service to Philadelphia. The postal department discovered that the delivery to Philadelphia by truck was almost as fast and a lot cheaper by truck. It was not the only mistake we made. The transportation back and forth to the offices of Dan Flood by his aide, was never paid for. The rates we charged for radio and mechanical services made some money, but not enough. I will say that Gene Schlenger worked for us at a very low salary. His automobile business had to support him. If he left, I did not have the time from my other businesses to operate the service. Neither did any of the other investors. We figured that we would check Allegheny Airlines and undercut their prices and still make money. Allegheny became very interested in us and brought an action to put us out of scheduled business. As firm's attorney, I represented us before the FCC board. I thought that Dan Flood would take care of things. I suppose that he might have tried, but the fact that his office was getting free transportation left us with a weak witness. It wasn't the only case I lost. My father had told me that a lawyer who represents himself has a fool for a witness. He was right.

Away from the business affairs of our taxi airline we had some very interesting items in our trips. When I landed at Chicago's Municipal airport (Meigs Field) built over the water on the Lake, the wind coming down the runway was a hundred miles per hour. That made for a very short landing. I was instructed by the tower to let their tractor pull me into a tie-down parking spot which they did. When I was being tied down, the wind turned my plane so that my wingtip hit the front of the neighboring plane, which had a radar set in it. My wingtip did not appear damaged, but the neighboring plane had the radar set damaged. The airport manager tried to notify the owner who, apparently, had not signed in. A check of its license with Oklahoma City's roster of private planes showed it was stolen some months before. My convention meeting took several days. When I went back to the airport, the operator of the plane had not been identified. The airport still charged me parking fees even though I helped them find a stolen plane.

Returning from the Canadian World's Fair, I landed at customs in Massena, a town where there was a Triangle Shoe Store. The customs office was so seldom used that it took hours to find an inspector while my family and I had lunch in the town. The inspector decided that there must be something secreted on the plane or why would I land there. Private planes were authorized to cross there but rarely did. He found a bag of tools and took the plane apart. At 5:00 p.m. he said that he would put the plane back together the next day. I called Dan Flood's office. Someone there spoke to the inspector. He then went to work and by 10:00 p.m. had the plane back together. My lesson was not to fly into relatively small towns with rarely used customs offices.

My lesson from flying was that unless you had to have a plane for business, if you flew for pleasure it was too expensive. I kept the last plane I owned for recreational purposes. One notable trip was with Harvey Klein and his wife in both of our planes to the north of Quebec off the bay separating British Canada from the remaining French Islands of St. Pierre and Michelin.

The plane became a liability rather than an asset so I sold it and retired from the airplane business. I have flown since in plane rentals but was always worried when I was flying a machine not my own.

CHAPTER 7

On My Own
After leaving the Triangle Shoe Company

The Triangle Shoe Company needed new locations and moves from old ones. While I was with it, I was closing, buying and leasing more than 130 stores. The legal work was substantial. I developed my own construction company. I started with a mobile home park, built a Mt. Pocono vacation development, purchased many shoe stores from New England to Florida using an airplane to get from one place to another. Flight instruction at Chickashay, Oklahoma, came in handy. I joined as a charter member a new organization, the International Council of Shopping Centers, in 1957. That organization used my lease form as a standard one for years. I was invited to address a CLE course in Manhattan to New York lawyers most of whom had probably used my lease and fortuitously saved a lot of money accordingly. I had in all our leases clauses that rent would stop in the event of local stoppages. This came in handy and effectively saved us rent in our store on Fulton Street, Brooklyn, when a riot broke out after our district manager shot an attempted junior would be assassin who had attempted to kill him raising a pistol while the manager was behind the cash register. It worked effectively in Kent, Ohio, when our store was a short distance from where the National Guard troops were gunning down Kent University students causing the store to close.

I became one of the recipients of new FEMA mortgages which kept me and my company in business after the 1972 floods. All my mortgages were consolidated into 1 percent interest mortgages, which cut my required payments down substantially. The Narrows Shopping Center later lost its major tenants. I was protected from bankruptcy personally because of what Joe Savitz taught me in Rosenn's office. My father told me that competent lawyers do not necessarily make good businessmen since they are too careful, being aware of numerous risks. I believe that his warning did not apply to the people with whom I dealt during my life. There were, however, many exceptions.

The International Council of Shopping Centers was organized on New Year's Eve 1957–1958 at the Starlight Roof nightclub of the Waldorf Astoria in Manhattan. It had been the brain child of a commercial real estate salesman who lived in Larchmont near my sister's residence in the Greensburg section of Scarsdale New York. My sister, Nancy Klein, had been a teacher in Manhattan when she married Lester Klein, a well-known physician in the area. She gave up teaching and busied herself with community activities. In that way, she learned the occupations of many of her neighbors. I was still working for Triangle Shoe Stores and asked her to find potential sites. Triangle had purchased all the Royal Shoe stores in Manhattan and Brooklyn. They were quite profitable and easy to service and operate. Nancy introduced me to her real estate neighbor who had listings on a number of buildings. The one that intrigued me most was a commercial building west of Scarsdale that he proposed to turn into an enclosed mall.

I had no experience with this type of location, so we did not make a deal. He was kind enough, however, to come to Pennsylvania and look at the grocery-centered buildings which were starting to be built. He made a number of suggestions to change the layout, which I followed. We discussed the fact that there was no literature available to instruct the shopping-center builders as to proper layout, traffic control, etc., and to merchant's associations in joint promotions. He called me a few days later with a proposal. He suggested setting up an organization to be named the International Council of Shopping Centers. I was working for a shoe chain and spending my weekends and free nights at the law office I had been assigned to by Judge MacDonald to enable me to take the Bar exam. There was little time to even sleep and eat. I found a clerk of the works to supervise the construction progress and followed through on my mentor's advice as to which chains to visit for necessary tenants. Filling the center was not easy, but the contacts I made through soliciting retail chains to join the ICSC made the job easier. When we made the announcement on New Year's Eve, my center was complete except for Bergman's Department Store. We were addressed by a representative of Connecticut Life Insurance. They had made arrangements with the University of Connecticut to provide our organization with classroom dormitory rooms, and instructors for a full week of how to build lease and finance shopping centers. We had enrolled a hundred members and 100 percent agreed to go. None of us knew anything about shopping, centers, but all of us were convinced that they were the retail future.

This was heady news for me. I was at the bottom of the totem pole in the retail and construction business. I had not yet become a lawyer and was probably the least affluent member of our organization. I felt like I did my first day at West Point. These guys in that room were strong real estate people with millions of dollars available for major projects. I had noticed in the Army that at the poker games, the players with the most money going in came out the winners. However, almost all of my fellow students were willing to give me information that I could never have received elsewhere including how to raise the construction funds, the take-outs, and the leases.

The leases were my cup of tea. I had made up all the leases in the Triangle Shoe Company since I was assigned to our new location department and I had excellent help from the law office partners in writing new and improved leases. I was probably the first person in our organization to turn out both landlord leases and tenant ones. I was invited a few years later to address the New York Bar Association concerning the leases. The meeting was held at the Plaza Hotel, and I felt like I had been given a general's star. I felt that every lawyer in that room had a great deal more knowledge of leases than I could ever gain. The ICSC decided to publish it along with some of my comments in one of their brochures. I began to get queries from quite a few lawyers as a result. The leases saved the Triangle Shoe Company quite a bit of money. I had inserted in one of my clauses the provision that any interruption of business because of civil or military strife stopped the rent and common area payments. The insurance clauses had the same effect, but covered only the circumstances causing damage to the structure such as floods or fire. When the National Guard killed a student at Kent, Ohio, the Triangle Store across the street's rent stopped. When the Brooklyn riots caused blocks of stores to be closed at the intersection of Fulton and Nostrand Streets, the Triangle Store did not have to pay rent for the weeks the store was closed to the public. The same problem took place in Jersey City during riots, but that was not a clear case since the building was partially destroyed by vandalism. Insurance took care of that. The ICSC's first letter stands for *International*. A few years after our start, the officers decided that we could pick up some members in Canada. We met in Toronto. The Canadians could not have been more hospitable. I was lucky enough to sit next to a local lawyer by the name of Dione. The Quintuplets was a popular newspaper item and, in questioning him about them, he said that he had no family relationship with them, but was famous in Canada since he was the head of the political party which wanted to separate from the rest of Canada. He was to attend his party's meeting in Gaspé that week and invited my wife and me to attend the meeting. Since I had some free time on my hands and my plane at the airport, I accepted. Harvey Klein, a cousin of my wife, had his plane there as well. He agreed to fly up to Gaspe at the same time with his wife.

The conference was well attended. It appeared that the Canadian population was growing much faster percentagewise than the United States so that shopping center groupings in the centralized locations were looked at very fondly by the leading companies, banks, and insurance companies. This meant that we would soon have a lot more members and become really international. We went into that meeting with not much more than one hundred members. Today, there are more than thirty-five thousand and all over the world.

Out trip to Gaspe was uneventful except for the fact that it was instrument weather all the way. My plane was well-equipped for such a flight. Harvey's plane was not as well-equipped, but he was a better pilot. He beat me to our destination going on top of the clouds to my surprise. He did not speak French so that he did not attend the Separatist Conference. I had enough French as a language Wyoming Seminary taught me to understand a great deal of what was said at the meeting. I left the meeting feeling that the breakoff of the French section would be calamities for their economy and decided on the spot that to develop real estate there would be much against the odds of success.

We concluded our trip with a flight to the nearest hotel in Nova Scotia, which had air-conditioning. Wonderful scenery, but no place for one of our shoe stores. The ICSC needed to do a job in educating professional real estate people. In those days we would start looking for locations in Nierenstein map books. With the development of computers, the site searches became much easier and cheaper because of a program developed called "A Site to do Business." This gave you major indications of where business was being done. The construction of shopping centers required a great deal more since new patterns for shopping required study as to where the population changes would require markets. I was in no immediate danger of losing my job.

Epilogue

Abe Koff, my grandfather on my mother's side, was born in a little village south of Kiev in the Ukraine. His family name was Shaposnik, or Shoemaker, in both Russian and Ukrainian. I discovered this by speaking to the director of records in her Odessa office which was the government center for such purposes when the Ukraine separated from Russia. The director had been contacted by David Koff, a cousin, now a retired attorney, who prepared a family tree. She wanted to charge David a fee he felt was too high. She pointed out to me that there were no computers in 1872 when my grandfather was born. The records are still in existence but difficult to find and not necessarily accurate. The birth records show that Abe had a twin sister and that Abe was drafted into the Army at age thirteen or fourteen. The handwriting is not particularly clear. The Colonel I spoke with in New York was correct. The director had no records of Abe's cousin on hand but said that Shaposnik, meaning Shoemaker, was a relatively common name. The Koff at the end means "family of" and is part of Russian names. His families were Cohen's and his gravestone shows that. David had sent a letter to then retired

General Shaposnik to see if there was any family connection. The response was denial. However, he apparently came from the same or near village since he is listed in the same register. There are probably many people there with the same name. Army intelligence was more thorough than I could ever be. Abe had told me that he had a twin sister but had not seen her since he was a child.

After Abe became a civilian he looked around for a job. He went to Switzerland and Poland where he had been stationed for some time. He heard that there was a daughter of a wealthy wine merchant in Odessa available for marriage. He took the train there and went to work for her father. Abe and Rose were soon married and a year later produced a baby. The Czar at the time had trouble in the Ukraine and would authorize pogroms to satisfy the Ukrainian Cossacks' thirst for rape of Jewish women and theft of Jewish person's goods. His father-in-law had wine barrels made with false bottoms so that, by hiding the women of the family in them, they could escape the Cossacks who would pierce the top of the barrels with their bayonets. My great-grandmother took her newborn baby into the safe place. The amount of oxygen was not sufficient for the baby, and it died. My great-grandmother brought her second grandchild, Rose, to the United States in 1906. Abe had been sent to the United States in 1904 with the admonition to find a job, and he did. I was living in Kingston by the time I heard this story in the den of our house from my great-grandmother. She had bought a townhouse on Delancey Street when she arrived in the U.S. She died at age one hundred. Her daughter Rose, my grandmother, had predeceased her. Her house was located in an area on the lower East Side, which now houses the Henrietta Szold School. I visited her there several times. It was an easy subway ride from the train station, which we used when coming from West Point.

She was somewhat of a matchmaker, and she sent to me at West Point Henrietta Szold's granddaughter on a weekend. I was flattered, but there was no chemistry there, and I never saw the young lady again. She also had a good sense of humor. When I visited her one time, she greeted me with "Here comes the General!" I would answer her that I was a long way from becoming a General. "I meant General nuisance," she would say. We got along fine. Her cookies were delicious. My mother was very impressed with her and became in love with Hadassah, the organization that built a hospital in Jerusalem. It was in its infancy then.

My grandmother Rose ran a shop for knitting goods and sewing supplies on the first floor of her home on Hazle Street in Wilkes-Barre. Abe's shoe repair shop was in a small shed at the side of the building. He had a thriving business as a shoemaker and a good location since the area was ethnically Russian and Ukrainian. He could talk to the residents.

I loved visiting him when we lived on Terrace Street. He gave me a quarter to take his beer bucket down the street to a bar where he had a charge account, and bring it back to him. It was my rare source of income until my father gave me an allowance of a quarter per week. Supporting his wife and six children kept my grandfather busy and out of mischief. When his former girlfriend from Poland showed up bringing a child with her she claimed was his, my father arranged to send her away with a substantial monetary payment. Abe always denied that he fathered the child but not that she had been one of several girlfriends he had while in the Russian army. He loved both beer and vodka. When he could afford it he would pour himself a glass of vodka during an evening meal. I never saw any evidence of alcohol on him. He used a sugar cube when having tea and coffee as well. Eventually, he had to have all his teeth removed and wore plates for the remainder of his life. His oldest child was my mother. Ben was the first son, Meyer the second, Jim the third, Charlie the fourth, and Harold the fifth. All of them had interesting lives. The iconoclastic Charlie Koff left his high school in his junior year and ran off to New York where he picked up a job as a guitarist with one of Xavier Cugat's bands which was traveling the Caribbean on cruise ships. The family had no knowledge of where he was for years. He learned how to arrange music while on the boats and also learned to play all the other instruments as part of his education. When I was stationed at Fort Macarthur in San Pedro, I saw Charlie frequently. He told me that his musical learning was by getting lessons from professional players on 115th Street in New York. Gershwin was there but he learned more from Oscar Levant and Michael Vivesky who was an immigrant from Russia. Vivesky taught Charlie the twelve-tone system, which he learned from Tchaikovsky while a student in Russia. Charlie joined BMI when the music industry was organized into ASCAP. Charlie's arrangement of "I dream of Jeanie with the light brown hair" was in direct competition with ASCAP's musicians, so they barred him from joining the union. His jobs dwindled to the point that he could no longer make a living in New York. He moved to Los Angeles.

Before he moved to Los Angeles, he called me and asked if I wanted to go to the World's Fair, then in Long Island. I agreed and spent more than one day with him learning about the business of being a musician as well as the World Fair displays including the Trylon and Perisphere. I was so impressed that I continued my piano lessons with OslofI Trygvassen, a Norwegian pianist with a two octave reach. He trained me to where I had a recital which was attended by an admissions officer from Julliard. They accepted me.

My father had other ideas which had nothing to do with

music. He smelled a war coming up and was right as usual. Charlie died in his seventies of a heart attack, leaving a wife and daughter who became a leading person in the Herbalife Group in Los Angeles. Her husband was an agent for movie and recording stars. Before Charlie died, I was with him not as often as I wished to be. He had invited my wife and myself to one of his private jam sessions of which he had two or three per month. Each musician played every other musician's instrument in this session. They were prominent classical works for the most part and they were played perfectly. Charlie explained that he could not be an arranger unless he could play all the instruments in the orchestra. He had been hired as a ghost writer for the musical background of many movies. He asked me one day if my wife and I would like to watch him insert the music for *High Noon* in the studio. We went. I did not know that the musical background for films was not put in until the film was finished. With his reputation as an arranger, he did many of these films. The orchestra was a large one and had many of the same musicians from his jam sessions in it.

The recording went without a hitch. The musicians were directed to play the right notes for every bit of film being treated. The film was not shown during the recording, but the music was accepted without a hitch and with no previous practice by the full orchestra. The orchestra and the composer came up to his stand to thank him, and he glowed with satisfaction. He told the composer that the music was good but not as good as he could do. The film (made to) achieved an Academy Award. As a ghost writer, he was not mentioned.

Charlie visited me some years after I left the Army in Pennsylvania. Our flood in 1972, called Agnes, seriously damaged the Susquehanna River towns. He decided on the spot that he would write a symphony about the flood. I had a construction company at that time and as building a housing development on Route 196 halfway between the Tobyhanna Depot and Mount Pocono, across the road from Gamer Ted Armstrong's Radio Church of God. We expected that flood victims might be good customers. Many of them worked at the Tobyhanna Depot.

Charlie actually wrote the symphony and sent me the pages in order. I can read music, but this was an arranger's music with every piece with a separate page. He never finished it. I guessed that he was too ill to do it by then and I went to California to visit him. We had lunch on the pier in Venice, and he explained that he did not have the strength to finish it and hoped somebody would. He died a few days later. I sent my copies to his widow Anne. I have no information as to what happened to it.

Meyer had settled down in Ocala, Florida, where he was the manager of the Ocala Hotel. This hotel was purchased by my father, just before he visited me in Germany. He disliked airplane travel and used the train whenever he could. There was something wrong with a switch in the tracks near Ocala which would require several hours to fix. He said that he walked into town a short distance and spotted a For Sale sign on a large hotel on the square across the street from the courthouse and the Park in which it was located. He discovered to his surprise that the register had dates well before the Civil War and bore the name of numerous politicians of the day. Ulysses Grant was one of the names. The hotel had a large garden behind it and the railroad station stopped right behind the rear garden which had a path leading into the hotel's rear entrance. He immediately went across the street to the courthouse where he found the lawyer responsible for the sale and wrote him a check for the down payment, the price being less than he was willing to pay. His train was signaling to reboard, and he left Ocala without the papers he had from the lawyer because of the rush back. He told me about his recent real estate purchases, including the Ocala Hotel, but could not remember the name of the community or hotel. I asked him how he would find out. He said that he would know when his check was sent back cashed. He had a keen eye for real estate and changed the first floor into retail stores and the rear gardens into a parking lot. He had created a shopping center in a central location downtown worth many times more than the costs. Meyer was asked to run it. He did for several years successfully. Ruth Forman Koff, Meyer's wife, took to Ocala quickly. She was a beautiful woman who was well received in the town and played in the Little Theater. She felt that she could do better in Hollywood and left with Meyer puzzled about the whole thing. She had taken the family auto to get there. Meyer took a while to replace himself with a manager and used his personal motorcycle to travel. Their marriage was irretrievably broken, but Meyer decided that he would get a job and stay in California. He suffered a series of severe headaches, was diagnosed with a brain tumor, and died on the operating table.

The next one to die was Harold Koff, the youngest of the brothers. He had been an Army Air Corps officer during the Second World War and left the service sometime after the war ended. He married Dolly—the tax collector of Johnstown, Pennsylvania—and went into a commercial selling of paper goods with a Johnstown address. He did well at it but had a difficult time with Dolly who was inebriated much of the time. He had resurgent stomach pains eventually diagnosed as stomach cancer and died. His hospital was not far from the airport. I flew in to see him several times. He loved to smoke, had not done so for many years, but asked me to buy him cigarettes. He said that the tobacco would not be in his system long enough to damage him further. He was right and passed away soon. He left one son, John, who lives in the Pittsburgh area.

Jim died next in Wilkes-Barre. He had a profitable dry goods business, a son, and two daughters. The last to die was the oldest brother Ben. He had been a manager of a Triangle Shoe Store in Williamsport, Pennsylvania. While there, he hired a young local lady by the name of Fanny to work in the store, and they were married soon after.

Ben decided to change store locations out of the community and moved into the Finger Lakes area near Ithaca and ran a Triangle Shoe Store there. When Ben found a furniture store in Ogdensburg that he could build up, he left the chain and went into his own business. I was a Triangle district manager in that part of the States and made it a point to visit with them whenever possible. They had a lovely home, and his business prospered—as did his married life. They had three children, one of whom developed cervical cancer. With no medical insurance, very expensive treatments were required. Ben had no backlog of funds to cover the treatments but never asked for help from the rest of the family. He carried a floor plan with two local banks covering the same merchandise to raise the money. When the banks discovered the fraud, they gave him a few weeks to straighten things out or they would have him arrested. I was having lunch with my father in Kingston in the dining alcove when the phone rang and Edith, his housekeeper, transferred the call to him. My father's hearing wasn't the best, so I was privy to the whole conversation. When he discovered what the problem was, he asked Ben for the persons and telephone numbers of the two bank officers with whom he was dealing. He immediately called each of them and asked them what sums would settle the matter. It was well over $100,000—a lot of money at that time. He called his office to send the checks at once to the banks. He never collected a cent from Ben after that and never brought up the matter. When Ben's daughter died of the cancer, my father called him and told him that since he owned a family grave site in Swoyersville, Pennsylvania, he could have her buried there. Ben accepted.

Ben needed a job. He still had a family to support. Since he ran his furniture business so well, my father felt that his best bet was to become a salesman for a major furniture manufacturer. My father knew most of the businessmen in our area. He called the ones in the furniture business and asked them which firm was looking to expand to the West Coast. He found one and told Ben to interview with them. Ben did. He moved to California and performed an excellent job for them. He was able to live comfortably there. His wife Fanny took a job with Bullocks Department Store where she became manager of the fur department.

I was living in California then. Zelda wanted a sealskin coat. I had little money. Fanny waited until she had a suitable coat marked way down in price and arranged the sale. Her education in Williamsport paid off. Ben had a ninetieth birthday party given for him by the many friends he had made. He appeared remarkably healthy at that time. However, his age caught up with him and he was the last of the brothers to die. At this time, I am the oldest member of this generation of our Koff family to be alive. I think I'll stay around for a while to deserve the distinction.

Our Weiss family arrived in the United States on Thanksgiving Day at Ellis Island. This is the story of the move from Mihalovce (then Nujmehi) to where they are today. The following is the Eulogy by Rabbi Lisa Stern, his grandniece, at his 1987 funeral service:

I should not be the one standing here remembering Aaron Weiss, my grandfather, your friend, your father, your boss, your grandfather and great-grandfather. Many more eloquent than I knew Aaron well. Rabbi Baras, Rabbi Levitzky, politicians, writers—these people knew him, were associated with him. They should be standing here paying tribute to this great man. But they, too, are gone. Aaron's passing does truly mark the end of an era, for all of us. By the time I knew my grandfather, he was already a living legend, it seemed.

From my earliest consciousness, I remember my grandfather as a great man who was looked up to by others. As a little girl, I came to expect to hear his praises. "Your grandfather—what a gentleman, what a wonderful man." "Did you know that your grandfather gave such and such, helped so and so?" I never heard it from him. I heard it from the people who worked for him and with him—the people who knew him from his organizational work, from his community involvement. I remember when I took a friend of mine to visit Grampa about ten years ago. "He's such a small man!" my friend commented. Small?! *I was shocked. For in my mind, Grampa Aaron was larger than life. He was a giant, a man who took giant steps his whole life, from an impoverished childhood in Austria-Hungary to a position of great prominence in this community.*

Aaron Weiss was born in 1894, and in 1906 at the age of twelve he came to the U.S. with his mother and five siblings. It was a story with which we, his family, were quite familiar, for every Thanksgiving, Grampa would stand and recount it for us. Often, one or another of the kids or Tess couldn't resist a quip or a side comment and Grampa would stop and glare and we would coax him back to his story. Now many of us are retelling Grampa's story to our children on Thanksgiving, but I thought he would like it if I shared his words at this time.

"The procedure for immigration in 1906 was similar to what we have today; namely, that every would-be immigrant is examined—not only as to his health and moral outlook, but also as to his financial status, as to whether he could take care of himself

financially, or someone would agree to assume that obligation if he was not fortunate enough to be able to earn his own living.

"In our case, we faced a unique problem. It took us almost two years to accumulate enough money and to prepare for the trip to America. Finally, about a month or two before leaving, we received a postcard from Uncle Schwarz (mother's brother) asking "What is holding you, why this delay?" He was wondering whether something had developed which would interfere with our trip. This card was thrust aside and forgotten. Finally, we left for America by way of Liverpool. Upon our arrival in Liverpool, the American examiner asked mother whether she had anyone in America that would assume responsibility for her. "Of course," she said. "I have a brother and a son, both of whom will assume responsibility for our well-being." Then he asked a very critical question, "What proof have you?" "Proof," she said, "I don't have any proof, but I know that they will, there is no question about that." He said, "I am sorry, madam, but we have no authority to let you go through, unless we have some definite proof, some mail or other evidence that we will not be burdened with you and your five children. I cannot let you go, we will have to send you back."

"What followed is indescribable—the crying and the screams were heartbreaking. Mother and the children were thoroughly frightened. Return to where? Nothing was left behind. We did not have a soul there—we did not have a penny that we could get. It was really a heartbreaking situation which seemed most desperate. Suddenly, something happened that is most unusual—this examiner turned to mother and said, "Let me see your baggage." She showed him the various items and he started going through them until, suddenly, he felt a piece of paper which happened to be the postcard from her brother. He turned to her and said, "This is all I need," and off we went to the U.S., not knowing that we would reach America on Thanksgiving Day."

I remember what used to astonish Grampa every time he told that story was the unexpected kindness of the stranger. And in truth that was what always impressed him most. His favorite stories were about the unexpected kindnesses and generosity of others.

He never took them for granted. He himself was renowned for his generosity—but he never failed to be amazed by his good fortune when someone extended themselves to him. Miracles, to him, were the people who helped him along the way.

This quality of his—a sense of appreciation and gratitude—was extended toward the country itself. For Aaron, America truly was the land of opportunity. He loved this country, the place where his dream had become reality. And he never took the freedoms secured by this country for granted.

In 1916, Aaron graduated from University of Pennsylvania Law School. He spent three years in the Navy as a radio operator. I must add that he heard the original broadcast of the Balfour Declaration.

In 1924, Aaron married Tess Koff. They were married for fifty-one years, and it was an extraordinary partnership. She equaled his drive and energy and ambition, in her own way.

They were both leaders—Tess with her charm and presence and charisma, and Aaron with his elegance and intelligence. Together they created a home that became a gathering place for friends, associates, leaders of causes, and great men and women. Most important, they created three children: Norman, Herbie, and Nancy.

Aaron was proud of it all. He was proud of Tess and proud of his children and proud of his success. He was proud of being a Jew— proud of his participation in the establishment of the State of Israel. He was proud of what he did to save other Jews, and he sponsored many who came to this country because he never forgot his own luck. With energy and certainty and confidence, he accomplished whatever it was he set his mind to do, and he had reason to be proud of his accomplishments. The backbone of it all, of course, was Triangle Shoe. "My Grampa is a shoe salesman," I used to tell people, before I understood the size extent of Triangle—136 stores at one time! But he was. When he took me in the store, he'd try shoes on me himself. He saw no distinction between himself and those who worked for him, and they loved him for it. He was respectful, appreciative and unpretentious. "Who do I have to impress?" he would have said.

There was another backbone: Edith. For fifty-one years she has cared for, cooked for, and looked after the Weiss family. Aaron and Tess would not have accomplished all that they did without her.

And he was impatient, stubborn. Many of us here have inherited that quality which so infuriated us—his certainty that he was right—that "Hungarian temper," as we called it. He was a man of indomitable will. Sometimes he was wrong, but he never knew it—but gracious always, and loyal. He was a lion and yet, it is also true to say he was essentially a private man. He had simple tastes: cereal and fresh-squeezed orange juice. Often he was quiet while Tess held court. But it was always extremely important to him to be a gracious host. I remember him writing dinner guests' names and professions down on a piece of paper before the party, to enable himself to be the consummate host.

And yet, honest— at the end of the evening he would say to his guests: "I always have a glass of hot milk before I go to bed. Would you care to join me?" He let you know it was time to go. There are countless anecdotes—each one of you has your own—stories which illustrate his impeccable honesty, his penetrating mind, his instinct for justice, his penchant for simplicity. And there are the organizations: Wilkes College, Mercy Hospital, United Jewish Appeal, Zionist Organization of America, Jewish Theological Seminary, Temple Israel, Development Fund of Wyoming Valley, all of these deserve to be mentioned, all of these were part of who Aaron Weiss was and of what made him great. And he is part of who we are.

Norman, Dad, Nancy—I know that Grampa was not the easiest of fathers. He was impatient, he had high expectations. And he himself set a standard of excellence and commitment that makes us all feel a little humbled. But at the same time, his best qualities live on in you—his humor, his generosity, his keen intelligence. He also gave you a great sense of pride in which you are a sense of pride we all share. He was the best father he knew how to be—and you knew that and loved him for it. And I think you knew he loved you.

None of us is surprised that Aaron has died. He was a very old man; he lived a long and full life. And yet, I know that there are those of us here who never really thought he would die. We suspected he would live forever, that he would fight off death itself the way he fought off the flood; the way he fought off his childhood poverty; the way he fought off set-backs and disappointments.

He was a fighter, and we learned that, too. If we have succeeded in inheriting even in small measure his honesty, his loyalty, his generosity, his human decency, then he will have won after all. He will have conquered death itself for we immortalize him by who are. My grandfather was a great man—a giant, after all. I loved him and was proud of him.

May his memory continue to be, for us, a blessing.

Eulogy for Aaron Weiss

Thursday, April 9, 1987

I visited Mihalovce in 2008. I had rented a car and driver for the day. The city had grown beyond my wildest expectations to an industrial complex with dozens of apartment and factory buildings in the town. Stalin had redeveloped it. He felt that the city was an outstanding example of what communism can accomplish. The old Jewish section was gone along with the synagogue. The graveyard was intact but overgrown with heavy grass and weeds. My grandfather, Menachem Mendel Weiss, was buried there in 1905. The gravestones are all identical and extremely difficult to read. The cemetery was in better shape and larger than I had imagined. My guide told me that it had been abandoned after the Second World War and that the oldest graves dated back to the 1400s. The population came from northern Spain having been chased out by the royalty since Jews were not allowed to remain there unless converted to Christianity. There was a castle in town which, although built in several different periods, had many of the same features of 46 East Dorrance Street, Kingston, Pennsylvania. It probably was the reason that my father was in love with the property he had bought from Ann Dorrance in 1938. The nearby village where the Weiss Inn that my father visited every weekend has disappeared. The family, much of which visited us when we lived in Wilkes-Barre, had moved to Budapest where they all perished. It was one of my saddest days.

Tess Weiss has been described under the Koffs above. She was active as a Koff and more active as a Weiss. She received the honor of Community Person of The Year in 1975. She was active in non-Jewish affairs having been in leading positions in the Campfire Girls, the Girl Scouts, many community charities, and on The Fox Hill Golf Course, where a tournament was held each year in her name. I was invited to pay for the prize each year which I was happy to do. She was very important in my life having educated me in subjects mothers generally do not get into such as boxing, golf and tennis. As a Phys-Ed teacher in the Wilkes-Barre School system, she had me schooled from age three to read, swim, play tennis, and basketball. She would not allow me to play football on Wyoming Seminary's team, but I was selected team manager by my classmates who were playing. Prof. Brace, our coach, did not like the idea. He went along with it anyway. Since he was also my math teacher he tutored me with dozens of math problems taken from years of previous West Point exams. Every question I had on that exam had been addressed by him which made the exam quite easy to answer.

Our Weiss family was made up of more Weiss uncles, cousins and aunts. My father's oldest half-sister from his mother's first husband had married out of the faith and was consequently declared to be dead by Jewish law. Her husband was an Ecker. She had children, but they were disowned as well. She moved to New York. Her son Richard became a dentist, lawyer, and National Bridge Champion in the finals held in Atlantic City. I was allowed to witness the final hand, but not knowing the game, I was hopelessly confused. I grew up having my teeth taken care of by him. I was never told that Rose Ecker was a real aunt and her son my cousin. Evelyn Sondheim gave me the information at Rose's funeral. I met cousins there I never knew I had. They were Presbyterian, and my father did not want it known. After all, he was an Over Seer of the Jewish Theological Seminary, President of Temple Israel, and an officer of the Jewish Community Center in Wilkes-Barre. Richard Ecker not only took care of my teeth, but he spent several hours with me demonstrating how he traded stocks on exchanges on volume figures alone. I followed his method for a while, and it worked better than I had anticipated. I have stopped trading stocks, but I feel that his method still has merit.

Morris Weiss was my father's brother and his closest friend. When Morris's wife died, his youngest son Stanford (Sandy) came to live with us in Kingston, Pennsylvania. Sandy was one year behind me in school. He made new friends quite quickly. It was pleasant having him in the house. My brother Herb and I were frequently bickering. Sandy acted as a pleasant intermediary. I left our house in 1943, having graduated from prep school, and entered the Army at West Point two months after my seventeenth birthday. Ben Weiss was another uncle who had a Boston Shoe store in Coatesville, Pennsylvania. He did not get along with my father who conveyed one-third of the Triangle stock to him on condition that he never enters a Triangle store. The conveyance was ordered by my grandmother at a family meeting in Pottstown where she ruled the roost. Triangle was already a successful chain, and she wanted it held equally. The fourth brother Tom was born with a cleft lip and speech impediment, which was probably not treatable in those days. She decided that Tom would become a tailor like his father. He did and spent the rest of his life in Pottstown.

My father's oldest Weiss sister, Goldie, married Ben Berger who set up a shoe store. Sam Feurman was a half-brother who had a jewelry store in Pottstown. He was a skilled watchmaker and delighted in taking a clock apart and seeing whether I could put all the parts together. His was a test I never passed. It was good training for stripping down weapons and putting the parts back in them clean. At the hundredth anniversary of my namesake ancestor grandfather, Harold Berger, a cousin who had married Loretta Schwartz (another cousin) arranged a party in one of Pottstown's parks and made out a family tree. I was surprised at the size of the party but delighted that he had done it. At the park, I met dozens of cousins I never knew before.

In 1956, I was given permission from Pennsylvania Chief Supreme Court Judge McDonald to take substitute legal education by studying on a clerkship basis in a local legal office. The office of Rosenn, Jenkins, & Greenwald offered to do the job. Harold Rosenn was assigned the job of my supervisor. I was allowed to do this provided the local bar association approved it. It did. I had completed approximately two years of night school training at Loyola Law School in Los Angeles while I was stationed as a Captain in the U.S. Army at Fort MacArthur in San Pedro. My duties there were unusual since my assignment was a special one.

General MacArthur had organized within the army a detail to be parachuted into North Korea to set up and operate an oil depot to support South Korean and U.S. Army troops in an invasion of the Chinese mainland. He had planned to surround the Chinese by moving across the Korean peninsula and accomplished that by landing forces at Inchon and cutting the Chinese off from their home bases. Since I had become a paratrooper after graduating from West Point and had no troops to command at the moment, I was assigned with three others to Caven Point, New Jersey, to learn how to run an oil depot.

After training at this facility, I was assigned to the Standard Oil Company of New York for practical training in overseeing depot operations. I was then sent to the Pacific Coast preparatory to going to Korea where some of my West Point classmates were already serving. However, President Truman learned of the planned but unauthorized Chinese invasion and fired General MacArthur. I stayed in New York City for a few days while the Army decided what to do with us. I watched General MacArthur in his ticker tape parade reception before I left the city. I knew General Hayden in charge of Fort MacArthur personally since he was one of my West Point teachers, and was delighted to be assigned to him.

I was put in charge of supervision of the operation of the Wilshire Oil Depot Company from which our fuel was being shipped to Korea through the Time Oil Company. My duties were basically clerical and I was allowed to leave the post each evening, which made it possible to enroll in Loyola of Los Angeles law school.

The night law school class was limited to a hundred. It was then the only accredited one in the State of California. I apparently was doing well enough academically so that after the conflict in Korea slowed to a stalemate, I decided to leave the Army.

The dean offered to transfer my grades to St. Johns' University in Brooklyn where Peter Paul Olszewski, a friend at Wyoming Seminary, was a student. My problem was how to support a wife and two children with no income. As a regular officer, I had no retirement claims, and I had no way to make a living, let alone attend law school. I took the only job available to me—selling shoes in a Triangle shoe store and working on commission. It was an employment ladder I could climb, but I did not want to be a shoe clerk and even a shoe store manager the rest of my life. I did not feel that I could achieve the standard of living I wanted in the Army and decided that I had to have a profession. Al Danoff, an old friend, suggested to me that Judge MacDonald was in town and might let me take the bar exam because of my military service and academic background. I visited him in his office and was pleasantly surprised when he offered me the chance to take the bar exam after a four year period of clerkship. No one was more grateful when I passed the bar exam in Philadelphia. Before I went down I was told that no one had passed the bar without a college post graduate degree since 1926. Smarter and better lawyers, including the ones that were at my bar exam being honored at the fifty-year Bar Association Dinner, were also being honored. After entering the legal profession, I had to decide what to do with my new title. Within twenty-four hours of my notification of passing, I had a client visit me with a family law matter. The case was settled satisfactorily because I had the experience of Rosenn's office. But my primary purpose was not to change the law, better it, or use it for devious purposes. I needed it to make a living and it did. I knew that the practice of law would educate me in certain business fields, and I decided to apply it to the real estate business.

Susan and Judd Shoval
Judd was an Israeli attorney. My daughter, Susan received the
highest grades at College of Insurance. She met Judd while taking
her third year in College at Hebrew University in Jerusalem.

Please join us in celebration of

Ruth Forman Koff's Life

1915 - 2010

April 16, 2011
2:00 to 4:00 p.m.
2900 North Flower Street
Santa Ana, California 92706

Sharing of memories
is most welcomed

RSVP prior to April 11, 2011
Sheila Koff, 949-675-3955

Meyer and Ruth Koff in 1934

ROSE SAPOSHNIKOFF AND DAUGHTER THERESA CIRCA 1905
(UNSUBSTANTIATED)

Photo made in Odessa. Tess Koff was 3 years old.

Victor Burr

Mr. Heard:
Not often does one meet a group
of youngsters
So well informed or able in de-
bating
A question of much weight.

Mr. Saw:
They were a credit to an institution
That is an equal credit to the
people
Of this community. Its aim is
lofty.
And it with pride may point to
service rendered
That to the future gives a guaran-
tee.

* * *

Last Friday is was my privilege to
serve as one of the judges of a debate held in the chapel of the Wyoming Seminary between debaters
chosen from the Independent and
Amphictyon groups. The other
judges were the Reverend Howard
R. Harrison, of Nanticoke, and Superintendent John B. Kennedy of the
Kingston schools. Mr. Kennedy
acted as spokesman for the judges.

* * *

The subject debated was—"Re-
solved: That Asia Should be Gov-
erned by Asiatics." Debaters for the
Independents, who upheld the affirmative, were Irwin H. Hertz and
Robert N. Smith, with John E. Whalen ready as alternative; supporting
the negative for the Amphictyons
were Ernest U. Buckman, 2nd, and
Norman E. Weiss, with Edward T.
Klett, Jr., in reserve as alternative.
Rebuttal was handled by Mr. Weiss
and Mr. Buckman for the negative—
by Mr. Smith and Mr. Hertz for the
affirmative. All were masterful.

* * *

Of course the judges of a debate
do not concern themselves with the
merits of the question, but only
with the merits of the debate. And
making choice among the debaters
at the Seminary on Friday was a
job that required thought and nicety
of judgment. Naturally the judges
sat in different sections of the chapel,
and had no contact with one
another while scoring their points.
Happily their decision agreed in
giving victory to the debaters for
the negative, and in declaring Norman E. Weiss the winning individual debater. A prize of $25 went
to Mr. Weiss.

* * *

But the members of the losing
team had every right to feel that
theirs was defeat with honor.
Listening to them I found myself
murmuring: "Cato, thou reasonest
well." They met the question
squarely, supported the affirmative
side of it effectively, and, while
always well-poised and confident,
were never offensive. It was a high
compliment to the winners that the
judges were unanimous in thinking
that they had a shade the better of
the debating. It reflects no discredit
upon the other debaters to say that
Mr. Weiss was especially impres-
sive.

* * *

Dean Adams presided with the
kindliness and gentility character-
istic of him. In making the awards
Superintendent Kennedy paid a fine
and deserved tribute to those who
had coached and counselled the debaters. With the sportsmanship to
be expected of them the losers con-
gratulated the winners, and with
the modesty of true gentlemen the
winners received the congratulations. Everything was exactly as
everything should be on such an
occasion. There was no failure at
any point.

* * *

Contributing superbly to the
musical part of the program were
Lorraine E. Polley, Nancy K. Jones,
and June Drendall. I was glad that
I was not required to judge among
these, for all performed so admir-
ably that a choice would have been
difficult. Each played the piano.
Miss Polley's selections were "Fan-
fare" and "March in G." Miss
Jones played "The Sadness of
the China Seas." The choice of Miss
Drendall was "Polonaise, E Flat
minor." The musical part of the program was as excellent as the rest
of it.

* * *

Always I find delight in a visit
to the Wyoming Seminary. President Fleck and Dean Adams are
among the friends I cherish most,
the teachers are admirable in every
way, the students are fine to the
core. The atmosphere is wholesome
and invigorating, the surroundings
pleasant to eye and ear. On Friday
I met Superintendent Kennedy for
the first time, and this in itself made
my journey to Kingston worth
while. The Reverend Mr. Harrison
I had met before, but this made all
the keener my pleasure at meeting
him again. Taking part in formal
judgment of a debate is a task to
be considered seriously, particularly
when the debaters are so evenly
matched. Nevertheless my answer
is "Yes" to any call made on me for
service at the Wyoming Seminary.

* * *

With equal heartiness I congratulate both winners and losers in Friday's contest. Splendid were they
both.

* * *

First competitive debate at Wyoming Seminary.

Times Leader
School debate in lieu of final oration, 1943

The Koff family — 1939

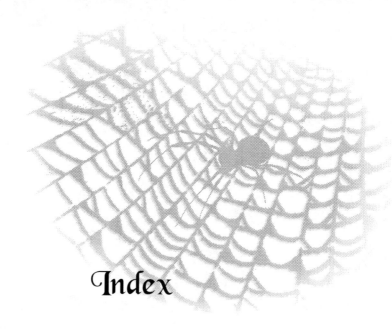

Index